DEBORAH BRUCE

Deborah Bruce has been a theatre director for twenty years and has now started writing. Her other plays include *Godchild* at the Hampstead Theatre, and *Same* for the National Theatre Connections Festival 2014. *The Distance* was a finalist for the 2012–13 Susan Smith Blackburn Prize.

T0347680

Other Titles in this Series

Deborah Bruce

THE DISTANCE

NICK HERN BOOKS

London

www.nickhernbooks.co.uk

A Nick Hern Book

The Distance first published in Great Britain in 2014 as a single edition paperback by Nick Hern Books Limited, The Glasshouse, 49a Goldhawk Road, London W12 8QP

The Distance copyright © 2014 Deborah Bruce

Deborah Bruce has asserted her moral right to be identified as the author of this work

Cover image: © Shutterstock.com/Rachata Sinthopachakul
Cover design: Ned Hoste, 2H

Typeset by Nick Hern Books, London
Printed in Great Britain by Mimeo Ltd, Huntingdon, Cambridgeshire PE29 6XX

A CIP catalogue record for this book is available from the British Library

ISBN 978 1 84842 444 9

The Distance was first performed at the Orange Tree Theatre, Richmond, on 8 October 2014. The cast was as follows:

BEA	Helen Baxendale
ALEX	Emma Beattie
DEWI	Daniel Hawksford
SIMON	Timothy Knightley
KATE	Clare Lawrence Moody
LIAM	Bill Milner
VINNIE	Oliver Ryan
Director	Charlotte Gwinner
Designer	Signe Beckmann
Lighting Designer	Stuart Burgess
Sound Designer	Max Pappenheim

For Ruth Bennett, Charlotte Garrard and Ruth Grey

Characters

DEWI, *forty*
KATE, *forty-one, Dewi's wife*
ALEX, *forty*
BEA, *forty*
VINNIE, *forty-three, Dewi's brother*
LIAM, *fifteen, Alex's son*
MAN, *late thirties*

Note

The design of the play should accommodate the Skype call in Scene Six being projected somehow so Simon and the children's faces can be seen by the audience.

A forward slash (/) in the middle of a line denotes an overlap in dialogue.

This text went to press before the end of rehearsals and so may differ slightly from the play as performed.

Scene One

A blank functional hotel room.

A MAN *sits on the edge of the bed.*

BEA *stands near the door.*

There is luggage on the floor.

BEA. I've changed my mind.

MAN. Okay. That's a shame.

BEA. I'm sorry.

MAN. It's okay. Have I done something wrong?

BEA. No, not at all. It just feels, different, in this small room. Being alone with you.

MAN. Of course, I understand.

BEA. It's not you. I'm sure you're very nice.

MAN. I'm quite nice.

BEA. I know you're not going to murder me or anything!

MAN. I'm pretty sure I won't.

BEA. I.

MAN. I mean I've never murdered anyone before –

BEA. No, it's just –

MAN. Of course, it could be that all first-time murderers think that.

BEA. I really don't think you're going to murder me.

MAN. Good. Well, I trust you. (*Pause.*) Look. It's fine. Let's go back to how we were. That seemed to be working well.

BEA. No you take the room –

MAN. We can go back to those hard seats in the departure lounge and maybe grab another coffee from that machine. It's only, what, seven hours till check-in. The time will fly by. You can entertain me by juggling some small milks.

BEA. I'm sorry. You think I've led you on.

MAN. No, I don't think that. I'm only joking. We're in a room. There's a bed in it. We're both tired after the flight, we should sleep. We've ruled out the murder thing.

BEA. I find. I feel that I've made a mistake.

MAN. No mistake.

BEA. I feel unsafe. And –

MAN. Okay. You are not unsafe. Baffling you with double negatives there. You are safe with me.

BEA. I feel lost.

MAN. You are tired.

BEA. I don't know where I am.

MAN. It's disorientating. We're halfway between two solid places. You are, literally, in Kuala Lumpur. I know you know that. It's kind of meaningless. Look. You are in a room with a very reliable, trustworthy guy. I'm an architect. I play tennis. I'm the oldest child in a large family, I am the very embodiment of responsibility. You are entirely safe here.

BEA. Sorry.

MAN. Look. Let's. I'll go and get another room. How about that?

BEA. No.

MAN. I'll go and get another room, maybe just down the corridor, maybe the one next door is free. I could dump my bags in it and then maybe we could just chat. In your room. Or you could come to mine? It was really nice talking to you before. We were getting on quite well, weren't we?

BEA. Yes.

MAN. Okay. Well, shall I go and see if they have another room?

BEA. The queue was quite long.

MAN. It might have gone down by now.

BEA. It was really long behind us.

MAN. I don't expect anything. I just liked you.

BEA. Don't you like me any more?

MAN. No, I've gone off you now. No, I'm joking. Of course I like you. (*Pause*.) Come here.

> BEA *moves into the room a bit*.

BEA. The nearer I get to you, the more like a stranger you seem.

MAN. Okay.

BEA. It felt different on the plane, and in arrivals. With lots of people about. But now there's no one else here.

MAN. Shall I go and see if some of them would mind popping back?

> *Pause*. BEA *stands in the room*.

BEA. I feel like I'm a stranger. In a room with a stranger.

MAN. Okay. Is that a bad thing?

BEA. No.

MAN. We strangers are famous for our particular brand of kindness. It is often remarked upon, in fact. Shall we stick with it and see how it goes?

BEA. Okay.

MAN. Okay.

> BEA *moves to* MAN *and sits beside him on the bed*.
>
> Hello, stranger.
>
> *Blackout*.

Scene Two

Large sitting room in KATE *and* DEWI*'s house, just outside Brighton.*

Early evening.

BEA *sits in the middle of the sofa motionless, still in her coat, with a glass of water. As if in some sort of shock.*

ALEX *sits on the arm of a chair.*

DEWI *hovers in the doorway. He has a muslin over his shoulder.*

KATE *stands in the centre of the room. The air is thick with some horror.*

KATE. We are all here. We are here for you, Bea. We want to do everything, and anything we can to help you get, Nat's so sorry she can't be here. She's gutted. Totally. Isn't she, Alex?

ALEX. Yes.

KATE. She's emailed through a whole load of paperwork, about custody laws, and Family Law Something. Have you got the printouts please, Dewi?

DEWI. They're on the kitchen table.

KATE. It's all printed out, we can call Nat if we need to, she's at the end of the phone. It was just that Pete had said he could have the kids, and then at the last minute there was a meeting he had to, he wasn't going to be back in time. Pete let Nat down basically. She ended up having to pick Connie up from karate, and taking Billy to his rehearsal for a dance show for Harriet Harman. At the same time as doing some other complicated. And Pete had said he could do it but at the last minute. And so, she really wanted to be here, she's going to phone later, she's emailed the custody. Laws.

Bea, do not worry. We are going to sort this out.

BEA. I'm fine.

KATE. Aren't we, Alex?

ALEX. We are going to absolutely.

KATE. We are going to get your boys back. (*Starts to cry.*) And Dewi's made a lasagne!

DEWI. Yup.

KATE. And you can just relax, we'll wrap you in a blanket and we will look after you. We are going to look after you, Bea. This is going to get sorted.

ALEX. Jesus Christ. This is so awful.

KATE. We are here. We are your friends and we are here.

Silence. KATE and ALEX look at each other. DEWI comes into the room.

ALEX suddenly moves towards BEA and sits beside her on the sofa and puts her arms around her.

That's it. Come on. Why don't you take your coat off, Bea?

ALEX. Do you want to take your coat off?

KATE. And your shoes. Take your shoes off, Bea.

ALEX starts to take BEA's coat off. KATE moves forward and takes off her shoes.

BEA. Thanks.

KATE (*to DEWI*). Get my slipper socks and the bottle of fizzy water.

DEWI goes.

(*Calling after him.*) And the printouts.

That's better.

ALEX stands and hands the coat to KATE who folds it carefully and unnecessarily. They look at BEA.

ALEX. God, you've lost weight.

BEA. Have I?

KATE. Yes you have.

ALEX. You are so skinny.

BEA. I don't think I have –

KATE. We are going to fatten you up.

ALEX. Like a big fat goose.

KATE. We are going to sort this mess out.

> KATE *starts moving furniture around. She moves piles of things off a coffee table.*

> I'm creating a work area. I'm moving these piles of things. Over here. We need to be *practical*.

> (*Calls.*) Dewi! What is he doing? How much do you bet he brings the bottle and no glasses? (*Calls.*) Dewi!

ALEX (*sits next to* BEA). I'm going to sit next to you.

KATE (*shouts*). Dewi!

> DEWI *appears in the doorway with the bottle of water and three glasses.*

DEWI. What?

KATE. Where are the printouts?

DEWI. I'm getting them. Stop shouting, you're going to wake Iris up. I'm getting them.

KATE. Well, I didn't know that.

DEWI. What did you think I was doing. Here's your water.

KATE. Oh, I see, you're just getting things one at a time. Thank you, Dewi.

DEWI. Shall I put the lasagne in now?

KATE. Isn't it in yet?

DEWI. Vinnie's back at eight so I thought we / could eat at eight.

KATE. Oh! As long as it's convenient for Vinnie!

ALEX (*to* KATE). Is Vinnie here?

KATE. Yes.

ALEX. Oh, right.

DEWI. He's building a summer house.

KATE *snorts*.

ALEX (*to* KATE). You never said he was here.

KATE. It's not the main event.

ALEX. What's he building a summer house for?

DEWI. To sit in. In the summer.

KATE. Which would be nice, only it's not really a summer house, Dewi's just calling it that because he doesn't want to tell you what it really is.

DEWI. What?

ALEX. What is it really?

DEWI. A summer house.

ALEX. Okay.

KATE. Oh right, a summer house, yes.

DEWI. It is!

ALEX. What is it really though?

DEWI. It's a fucking summer house.

KATE. It's a recording studio. For Dewi's / own personal use.

DEWI. For God's sake.

ALEX. Are you writing again?

DEWI. No!

KATE. As opposed to a summer house, for the whole family.

ALEX. Are you recording again?

DEWI. No! It's a summer house.

KATE. A summer house with soundproofing. In case anyone in the family turns the pages of their book too loudly and disturbs the neighbours. Whatever, Dewi. Printouts, please. And my slippers for Bea. Are you okay, Bea? Bea, I'm so sorry about this.

DEWI. Yeah. Sorry, Bea.

BEA. It's okay.

> DEWI *exits*.

ALEX. Is he writing again?

KATE. Sorry, Alex, I'm actually quite upset about this whole thing, it's been really a major, it's massive actually and it's connected to a whole load of other stuff, and the repercussions… I'm trying to forget about it so I can concentrate on Bea's much, much more serious situation, so I'll tell you later, if that's okay.

ALEX. Okay. (*Pause.*) It's weird you didn't tell me Vinnie was here though.

KATE. I've told Dewi not to let him come in here, while we're –

ALEX. It would have been nice to have had some warning.

KATE. While we're concentrating on Bea.

ALEX. No of course.

KATE. Sorry though.

ALEX. It's fine. Of course.

> DEWI *comes in with the printouts, he hands them to* KATE.

KATE. Thank you, Dewi.

DEWI. Lasagne's in.

KATE. Thank you, Dewi.

> DEWI *exits*.

(*Looking through the printouts*.) Okay, so. This is just a load of stuff about, oh I see what's she's done. This is stuff *specific* to Australia, Australia's Family Law Amendment, Australian Child Custody, Joint physical care, 65DAA, what the hell, okay, so this is going to be very useful. To have here. The main thing, Nat said was, about having to get you to write a statement, the problem with you having left the house, she said something about you leaving the family home, I think getting the plane, something about it being, not a *seriously* bad thing, just a tiny bit bad in terms of. Basically, what we need to establish is, how we can sort this out.

BEA *stands up.*

BEA. Can I go to the loo?

KATE. Oh yes, of course, that's totally. That's fine.

BEA *exits.*

ALEX *and* KATE *look at each other, make desperate faces.*

ALEX *gets up and goes to her bag.*

ALEX. I've just got to quickly call and see if Hal's alright.

KATE. Is he at Dan's?

ALEX. No, he's having a sleepover with this new boy. His mother's called, Frish, or something. (*Holds up her phone screen to* KATE.) How would you pronounce that?

KATE. Frishe? Are you sure you've spelt it right?

ALEX. God knows. And Benji's with Joel. It's his weekend.

KATE. Where's Liam?

ALEX. At home, don't say anything.

KATE. On his own?

ALEX. Yes, don't say anything.

KATE. God! –

ALEX. Don't –

KATE. What if –

ALEX. Honestly I can't think about it.

KATE. Okay. (*Pause.*) I'm sure he'll be fine. He's very mature.

ALEX. I'm going to text her, then I can just call her F.

KATE. You could have brought Liam with you.

ALEX. He wouldn't want to come, would he? He doesn't want to do anything. He'd have to speak to people. And walk along. He'd hate it.

KATE. One of us has to go back out to Melbourne with Bea. This is hopeless.

ALEX. Do you think?

KATE. How's she going to manage on her own? She can't even speak. It should be Nat really, only Pete's so *useless*.

ALEX. *God*. Isn't he?

KATE. She can't fight from here.

We have to be firm with her. She always seals herself off like this. We have to make her let us help.

ALEX. I don't mind going.

KATE. What about the boys?

ALEX. You can't leave Iris.

KATE. I probably could. For a week or so.

ALEX. Could Dewi cope for a week on his own?

KATE. He could always get his mum to come.

ALEX. You go then.

KATE. Yes.

ALEX. Say that to her when she gets back.

KATE. Nat can't believe that she's come over without the boys. She said it's *disastrous*, it will look *terrible* in court. Not only leaving the family home, but leaving the country. It makes it a hundred times harder, it's like she's given up on them.

ALEX. Of course she hasn't. Don't say that to her.

KATE. I'm not going to say it to her, I'm just saying it to you.

ALEX. It won't go to court.

KATE. It could easily.

ALEX. She's their mum!

KATE. She's left the country!

ALEX. Only temporarily. / To get her head together.

KATE. Simon can use it against her.

ALEX. I'm just going to call Liam, I'm still listening.

ALEX *makes a call.* KATE *looks through the papers.*

BEA *returns.*

She stands looking out of the window into the garden.

BEA. I love your garden.

ALEX (*on phone*). Hello, darling.

BEA. Thank you for that party, Kate.

KATE. Don't be silly.

ALEX (*on phone*). Where are you?

BEA. No, thank you for doing that, it was a lovely party, all my friends.

KATE. Pete lost his car keys. / What an idiot!

BEA. Such a send-off. I really believed I would never come back.

ALEX (*on phone*). There's food at home, Liam. Who are you with?

KATE. Well, you're not properly back yet.

BEA. You've got a lovely home.

ALEX (*on phone*). How long are you going to stay there? Did you lock the back door?

BEA. A family home. You've got proper things.

KATE. Oh, not really. It's all left-over tat from when Dewi was raking it in. Bea. Simon can't do this, you know. We're going to get those boys back. Listen.

ALEX (*on phone*). Ring me when you get home. Liam?

KATE. Me and Alex were just talking –

ALEX (*on phone*). Ring me when you get in though.

KATE. One of us, probably me, is going to come back out with you, okay?

BEA. Back out?

ALEX. Right, sorry about that.

KATE. I'm just saying to Bea, one of us, probably me, is going to come back out to Melbourne with her.

ALEX. Oh yes.

BEA. Why?

KATE. To support you. To sort this out.

ALEX. So you're not fighting this on your own.

KATE. Alex, your phone's / flashing.

ALEX. Oh God it's Frish, I have to get this sorry – (*On phone.*) Hi! Hi!

KATE (*to* BEA). She doesn't know her name! She wrote it down wrong!

ALEX (*on phone*). Hi, hi, how's it going? Is Hal being okay?

KATE. And I think we need to go as soon as possible, I'm not being funny, Bea, I know it's really hard and complicated, and you just needed to come home. Touch base briefly and sort your head, but it looks, a tiny bit, Nat said, you know, leaving the family home. (*Picks up the printouts, waves them around, puts them down again.*) Leaving the sort of country. I know you just needed to get your head together. But we need to get you back there. Quickly. With Kalan and Jay, where you belong. After the lasagne we should get online, book some flights. After the lasagne. And a big glass of wine.

ALEX (*on phone*). Aaaah, sweet. Thank you so much. (*Mouthing to* BEA *and* ALEX.) Sorry sorry.

KATE. Now. Are you booked on a return flight? Because we could transfer it sooner and I could just book myself on the same flight.

BEA. I'm not, no.

KATE. Oh, okay, well that's no problem.

ALEX (*on phone*). Yes please, thanks so much, Fri.

KATE. That makes it easier in fact.

ALEX (*on phone*). Hello, baby, are you having a lovely time?

ALEX *leaves the room.*

KATE. She'll be back in a minute. We'll get it all sorted out.

BEA. Right.

KATE. Dewi can manage perfectly well with Iris, Vinnie's here as well, not that he knows one end of a baby from the other, but. He'll be fine about it.

And it won't be for long, Simon's not totally unreasonable, is he?

BEA. No.

KATE. He's basically a nice bloke, isn't he?

BEA. Yes.

KATE. Obviously. You wouldn't have got together with him if. You wouldn't have had two children with him, would you? If he was a total monster? He'll *know*. He'll know that what he's doing is crazy. He'll know that he has to give you your boys back.

BEA *doesn't say anything.*

Surely. And if he doesn't, then you've got me there. And we'll go to the top lawyer and throw the, the keys, not the keys. What do I mean? My head is mashed potato. What do you throw at someone when you get a lawyer, you *know*.

ALEX *enters.*

Alex, what do you throw at someone when you get a lawyer?

ALEX. When?

KATE. You know, we'll throw the mmmmnn at him.

ALEX. What, like a custard pie?

KATE. No!

ALEX. The shaving-foam ones do you mean?

KATE. No! Of course not.

ALEX. Well, I don't know what you're talking about.

KATE. Nevermind. Je-sus.

It's a famous expression. Everyone says it.

I wish Nat was here.

Silence.

ALEX *and* KATE *look at* BEA. BEA *doesn't engage.*

So, anyway. Is Liam okay?

ALEX. I think so.

KATE. What's the matter?

ALEX. He's in Chicken Cottage in Peckham with a whole load of people. There's food in the house. There was no need for him to go out.

KATE. Oh.

ALEX. Have you said about going to Melbourne?

KATE. Yes I have.

ALEX. That's a good idea, isn't it, Bea?

KATE. I think it would be really helpful for you to have back-up. A witness.

ALEX. A friend.

KATE. Yes of course.

DEWI *stands in the doorway.*

DEWI. You all alright?

KATE. Yes thank you, Dewi.

DEWI. Anyone want anything?

KATE. We're fine, thank you.

ALEX. More wine please.

DEWI. Sure thing, anything for you, Bea?

BEA. I'm fine.

KATE. We're just in the middle of talking, Dewi, we're fine.

DEWI. Oh. Okay.

He goes.

ALEX. Why are you being horrible to him?

KATE. Ughhh.

ALEX. Are you having a row?

KATE. No, it's fine.

ALEX. Is it about Vinnie?

KATE. I'll tell you later.

ALEX. Is Vinnie with anyone?

KATE. Don't even think about it.

ALEX. I'm not asking because of that.

KATE. Honestly, Alex, you've got enough on your plate, he's a
massive child.

ALEX. I'm not asking because of that! I just wondered what he
was up to, is he still in Cardiff?

KATE. Why?

ALEX. I'm just interested –

KATE. Do not be interested in Vinnie –

ALEX. Not like that!

KATE. I knew this would happen!

ALEX. What? Nothing's happened. I'm just asking how he is.

KATE. He's living rent-free in his brother's house, probably
having ducked out of some messy situation with someone

else's girlfriend, probably owing someone a whole load of money and probably avoiding several attempts from the CSA to get in touch with him about a classroom of illegitimate children in Cathays somewhere –

ALEX. Illegitimate children? / Kate's in the 1950s!

KATE. And here he is building a recording studio that no one needs, unbelievably slowly, in the middle of my garden.

ALEX. Do you actually know any of that or are you just making it up?

KATE. I'm making it up. Based on the knowledge and experience that I have gained over the years living on the periphery of his grubby little life.

ALEX. That's really harsh. I thought he was sweet.

KATE. Yeah, he's sweet.

ALEX. He's not a bad person.

KATE. How are you measuring that? / He's hardly a good person.

ALEX. I like him!

KATE. That says more about you. / I'm sure he doesn't *mean* to ruin people's lives.

ALEX. What does that mean?

KATE. He's older than us, you know?

ALEX. Do you think I only like bad people?

KATE. Why are we talking about this? / Sorry, Bea.

ALEX. Paddy wasn't a bad person.

  KATE *gives her a look.*

  Joel wasn't a bad person.

KATE. Paddy just had a wife and two kids he forgot to mention –

ALEX. One kid. The oldest wasn't his.

KATE. And a serious coke problem, y'know, apart from that. /
Bloody hell, Alex.

ALEX (*laughing*). Oh, fuck off. Sorry, Bea. Sorry. Right, come
on.

KATE. Right. So you haven't got a return ticket. (*Looks at*
ALEX.) I'm going to go online and see what's available.

BEA. Dan was nice.

ALEX. Yes, thank you, Bea. Dan was nice.

BEA. Why didn't you stay with Dan?

KATE. Because he was nice?

ALEX. It just didn't work out, did it.

KATE. You hardly gave it a chance.

ALEX. Because I knew it wasn't right.

KATE. You didn't want Hal to have a live-in dad because then
Liam and Benji would feel worse about their dads not being
there –

ALEX. No –

KATE. That's what you said!

ALEX. It was a bit that. But I knew it wouldn't work anyway.

KATE. Why?

ALEX. He wasn't who I had thought he was, was he?

KATE. Who did you think he was?

ALEX. I don't know. I thought he had a poet's soul but he
didn't. Why are we talking about my mess, / we should be
talking about.

KATE. I know, sorry, Bea.

ALEX. What's happened, Bea?

KATE. Yes. I wish you'd talk to us.

ALEX. You don't have to / but.

KATE. You've done that thing you do. / When you shut down.

ALEX. You've gone all pale and flat, like you've been ironed.

KATE. You always do it. It makes you so difficult to help. And we can't help you if we don't know what's going on. Did he take the kids from nursery?

ALEX. Did he, Bea?

BEA. It wasn't that.

KATE. Where has he taken them?

DEWI enters with a glass of red wine and gives it to ALEX.

DEWI. Sure I can't get anyone else anything?

ALEX. Thanks, Dewi.

KATE. Just bring the bottle in and leave it here and then you don't have to keep coming in all the time.

ALEX. Aaah, poor Dewi.

KATE. Have you checked Iris?

DEWI. No, she's fine.

KATE. Did you take that cardigan off her before you put her down?

DEWI. No, she wasn't hot.

KATE. No, it's fine for a tiny baby to lie under two sheets and an eiderdown with a lambswool cardigan on, they recommend it apparently. For God's sake, Dewi.

KATE gets up and leaves the room.

There is a moment's silence.

DEWI. Just say if you want me to show you how to use the Skype on the laptop, I don't know if it's appropriate, but I thought. I don't know, maybe it would be weird for the boys to see you. But it's there. If you want to. If it's appropriate.

BEA. Thanks, Dewi.

ALEX. That's nice. That's thoughtful.

DEWI. You might need to close the curtains, if it's daylight. I don't know the time difference.

ALEX. Oh yes, the time difference.

DEWI. Yes.

ALEX. It's such a long way away.

BEA. Thanks. Yes I might.

DEWI. Okay. Whenever you like.

Pause.

ALEX. I'm sure Iris will be fine in her little cardi.

DEWI. She wasn't hot.

Pause.

BEA. He didn't take the boys. He didn't take them from nursery or anything like that. He's just with them, at the house.

ALEX. Okay. So. Is he holding their passports? Did he stop you from bringing them with you because you'd said it was over?

BEA. He didn't stop me from doing anything.

ALEX. So you said it was over, and that you were coming back to England, and what did he say?

BEA. I didn't say it was over, we both said it was over. We agreed it's over.

KATE *enters holding a baby's cardigan.*

ALEX. Because he can't stop you having the boys. / Bea, they're your boys.

BEA. It's not like that.

ALEX. They belong with you.

BEA. They're with their dad.

KATE. When you called me from the airport. When you were crying and saying, he's got the boys, I said to you, do not get on that plane without them, I really think you need to get back there as soon as you can, you don't know what he's doing, he could be taking them anywhere, he's got the boys, he's got their passports, you're powerless to do anything from here, Bea, you need to get back there and fight. I don't know why you're being so, so / passive.

BEA. I'm not going to tear them in half.

KATE. What do you mean?

BEA. It's not their fault I made a mistake.

ALEX. What mistake, when did you make a mistake?

BEA. He's a brilliant dad, the boys are his life.

KATE. Then you either have to stay in Melbourne, which isn't ideal but I suppose is an option, or commit to the next ten years of flying them backwards and forwards for holidays to see him, that's fine, that's to think about, but what's worrying me now, Bea, is you here, and the boys there, and Simon having all this time, stewing in his own juice, to get a head start and build up a case against you having them at all, and what we're saying is, you have to get back there to fight for these boys because worst-case scenario, I'm not trying to scare you here, Bea, but worst-case scenario is, you'll have a trickier legal battle on your hands to wrestle them back off him the longer you stay away. That's what we're saying to you. And Nat's worried about that too. In the printouts.

Pause.

BEA. I'm not going back.

ALEX. What, ever? (*Laughs.*)

BEA. We've decided.

KATE. Decided what?

BEA. He's better at it than me.

Silence.

It's decided.

Pause.

The alarm on DEWI*'s phone goes off.*

DEWI. Oh, that's the lasagne, it's not ready, I just have to take the foil off.

DEWI *exits*.

ALEX. Bea. What… Listen to me, okay.

KATE. Now look…

ALEX. It's hard, I know how, daunting it must feel, to – You can do this. Come on.

KATE. What do you mean, he's better at it than you?

ALEX. Come *on*, Bea.

KATE. God. I mean, God.

The front door opens and slams.

A moment later VINNIE *enters*.

VINNIE. Chaka Khan, Chaka Khan. Let me rock you Chaka Khan. Good evening, ladies.

KATE. Hi, Vinnie.

VINNIE. Good evening! Ladies! It sounded like. Like I had returned from some far-off land where there were no ladies and I had just discovered you, like Christopher Columbus. Ladies!

KATE. You know, Bea, and Alex, don't you, Vinnie?

BEA. Hi.

ALEX. Yeah, we met, at Kate's wedding, wasn't it?

VINNIE. Kate's wedding to Dewi?

ALEX (*flustered*). Wasn't it? She's only had one wedding, / haven't you?

VINNIE. I'm joking, of course we met.

ALEX. I was going to say!

VINNIE. Come on, how are you?

ALEX. I'm good yeah, I'm okay.

VINNIE. Sweet.

Pause.

KATE. Dewi's in the kitchen, taking some foil off.

VINNIE. Hey! It's all happening here.

ALEX. What you been up to?

VINNIE. Been up in London all day, meeting a man about a dog. Shit, that place stinks. Have you got the news on? It's all kicking off.

ALEX. Is it still? In Tottenham? Because of the guy the police shot?

VINNIE. It's going ballistic, they'll burn the whole place down with any luck.

ALEX. Don't say that.

VINNIE. You're okay here, you're well out of it.

ALEX. Yeah but my kids aren't.

VINNIE. No one can be bothered to set fire to anything here.

ALEX. Shall I put the news on? Where's the remote control?

VINNIE. It's moved into Enfield now. Where's that?

KATE. North.

VINNIE. A guy at Victoria said they were smashing up shops in Brixton.

ALEX. Fuck.

VINNIE. You fucking crazy Londoners. There was a girl with a baby in a pushchair smoking a spliff on the Tube. No one said anything, I was like, whoa!

ALEX. I'm pressing everything here. How do you get the telly on? I need an eight-year-old to operate machinery.

VINNIE. Give it here.

VINNIE *gets the TV on.* ALEX *and* KATE *look at each other. It's an advert. It's very loud. He turns it down.*

Have I got time for a bath?

KATE. Dewi's in charge.

VINNIE. How did that happen?

KATE. Just of supper. I'm still in charge of everything else.

VINNIE. I'm going to crack open a beer, anyone want one?

ALEX. What number's the like, non-stop news channel?

KATE. We're alright, Vin, can you close the door on your way
out?

*VINNIE exits backwards as if he had a gun and was on a
stake-out. He closes the door.*

Can you turn the telly off just while we have this
conversation? Liam's fine, he's nowhere near Tottenham.

ALEX. I'll watch it later.

KATE. Enfield's not even in London. Vinnie'll be exaggerating
anyway. God, he's such a twat.

ALEX turns the TV off and sits down.

KATE picks up the laptop.

Right, I'm looking at flights. Okay, Bea?

ALEX. It's going to be easier, isn't it, if Kate comes with you,
Bea?

BEA. I'm not going back.

KATE. Of course you are, I'm booking two flights. Sorry, Bea, I
have to overrule you here, you don't know what you're doing.

BEA. It's decided.

KATE. Nothing's decided, don't keep saying that.

BEA. We talked about it. We've decided. I know you're trying
to help me but this is the decision I've made. I am leaving
the boys in Melbourne with their dad. They'll have a
wonderful life. It's the best way. I made a terrible mistake.

ALEX. Kalan and Jay aren't a mistake –

KATE. How can you say your children are a mistake?

BEA. I was nearly forty, I was in a panic when I met him.

KATE. You were nowhere near forty. / You were thirty-six.

BEA. I was thirty-seven, you were all with people, or having kids. I wasn't with anyone, I'd been single for two-and-a-half years. I had no kids. I met him. He seemed kind.

KATE. It was more solid than that, you had *two* children with him.

BEA. I was in a massive panic. I couldn't see properly. It was all out of context. I should never have moved there. I can't work there. I don't like anyone. I can't fit in. No one knows me. No one can even pronounce my name.

ALEX. What? Bea?

BEA. Beatrice, they say Bea*trice*, they don't get me. I don't feel like me there.

KATE. I was forty, the sixth round of IVF.

BEA. I want to come home. I've made a mistake. Please, Kate, don't criticise me, / don't compare this –

KATE. God, Bea, you know how long Dewi and I –

ALEX. No one's saying you can't come home.

KATE. Ten years we were trying to have Iris. / You were in a panic?

BEA. Don't, Kate, I know that, it's different. / This is about me.

KATE. The thought, the idea that I would even consider for one second –

BEA. You and Dewi have been together for ever, it's not the same, / please don't.

KATE. It makes me feel physically sick, the thought of walking away from Iris.

BEA. I know.

KATE. Abandoning her. I am not going to let you do this.

BEA. I'm doing it. Let me do it. I'm not abandoning. It's for the best. It's what I want. (*Pause.*) I thought having babies would anchor me, stop me feeling so adrift. Why do I still feel so adrift?

KATE. Sorry, Bea. Sorry. But I cannot believe how utterly, unbelievably selfish you are being.

ALEX. Kate!

KATE. Sorry, Bea, but I don't recognise you. What about Kalan and Jay? You think this is what they want? You think that in years to come they are ever going to understand why their mother abandoned them? Have you thought about that?

BEA. Yes. I have thought about that. They can contact me, / I'm not abandoning them.

KATE. They can contact you? That's nice! You think this is what they want?

BEA. Yes. This is what they'd want –

KATE. Hello!

BEA. If they understood and had a choice, there's no way they would choose leaving their daddy, and their dog, and their home and their friends and their routine and their nana, to come to what? A flat in Finsbury Park with me.

KATE. They'd do anything to be with their mum.

BEA. To-ing and fro-ing on planes back and forth all the time, I'd be broke, I couldn't afford to do it, I haven't sold a painting for three years. How would we survive?

ALEX. You could stay at mine.

BEA. This is the best way.

KATE. You could come and live here. You could live in the summer house.

BEA. That's not what I want. I don't want to live in a shed in your garden / with two kids.

KATE. You could paint. It's not a shed. / Dewi could have the kids.

BEA. They're with their father. He wants them.

KATE. What, and you don't? For God's sake, Bea. I'm not accepting this.

BEA. Well, sorry.

KATE. I won't accept that you have thought this through / and come up with this. Alex?

BEA. You're not listening to me. / It is the best thing for them.

KATE. You have totally lost your mind. I would rather, cut – my – throat, than leave my baby on the other side of the world.

BEA. Cutting my throat would be easier.

KATE. Don't dress it up as some act of sacrifice. Alex, come on, say something. Help me here. She's gone mad, she's talking as if there are no choices.

ALEX. It is difficult to hear you say this stuff, Bea.

Pause.

BEA. I am asking you both, as my oldest, closest friends, to accept the decision I have made. And I am sorry if it is difficult to accept. I can assure you, it has been difficult to make.

KATE. Why didn't you talk to us before? While you were making the decision? Because you knew what we'd say, you know it's nonsense, that's why.

BEA *stands up.*

Where are you going? / Why are you standing up?

BEA. I can't talk about this any more at the moment.

KATE. What, so that's it?

BEA. Please, Kate. Don't criticise me. As my friend, just…

KATE. Just what? As your friend, what?

BEA. Trust that I have made the best decision. I don't want to fall out with you.

KATE. We have to talk about it, you can't bury your head. You absolutely need to talk about it or we can't help you.

BEA. Let me do this please, Kate.

KATE. I'm sorry, Bea. I can't do that.

ALEX. Okay. Let's, hang on, let's.

KATE. I can't stand by and watch you make a selfish, misguided, stupid decision that is going to cause two innocent children a lifetime of damage and pain. I'm sorry.

ALEX. Stop it, Kate. You're upsetting her.

KATE. Good. She's upsetting me.

ALEX. Don't.

KATE. I don't mean good, obviously.

Sit down.

BEA. I'm going out, I need to / get some air.

KATE. Don't be so ridiculous, we're in the middle of a / conversation.

ALEX. Let her go out if she wants to, / go on, Bea, it's okay.

KATE. We're in the middle of a – Oh go on, run away from confrontation as usual. My God, you're reacting like you did in the first year when we were trying to sort out that –

ALEX. Leave her alone –

KATE. Stupid house share –

ALEX. Don't harangue her!

KATE. We're supposed to be adults now!

ALEX. Let her go out if she wants to.

KATE. We're your friends, Bea, why did you come here if you don't need our help? It's our duty to stop you making this insane mistake, / it's our duty.

ALEX. She needs our support, Kate.

KATE. I'm trying to support her. Bea, just sit down.

BEA *moves to the door and exits.*

KATE *and* ALEX *sit in silence for a moment.*

KATE *suddenly picks up the laptop and starts to type.*

ALEX. What are you doing?

KATE. I'm booking two flights to Melbourne. She hasn't even got a fucking return flight. She left those two innocent boys there on a fucking single ticket to Heathrow. Can you believe this? Call Nat.

ALEX. Hadn't we just better wait for her to come back and talk to her again?

KATE. What's the point? She's not present in her head. She's in shock. She's having a breakdown. We have to take control, she needs us to.

ALEX. She won't like it.

KATE. I don't fucking care. I'm Kalan's godmother, for Christ's sake. If I can't protect him from being abandoned by his mother while his mother is in my actual house then, you know, what the fuck is going on? Call Nat.

ALEX. To say what?

KATE. To get her here. Fuck Pete and Harriet fucking Harman. (*Calls.*) Dewi!

DEWI (*offstage*). What?

KATE. Come here a minute.

DEWI *enters with oven gloves.*

What's Bea doing? Don't let her go out the house.

DEWI. She's in the garden with Vinnie.

KATE. Oh great! What have you left her with Vinnie for?

DEWI. They're having a cigarette, what's happened?

KATE. Don't let her go anywhere. Go and look in her bag and get her passport.

DEWI. Er. No.

KATE. I *need* her passport. Alex, you look. Thanks, Dewi, thanks for your help.

DEWI. It's all kicking off in London, I'm just listening to it on the radio. It's gone mental.

ALEX. What's happening?

KATE. Can we just concentrate on this, please?

DEWI. They're ransacking the place. They've set fire to a police car in Brixton. They've got the riot guys out. Supper's about twenty minutes.

KATE. Alex, can you go and get Bea's passport, please?

ALEX. God, I'm going to check Liam's gone home.

ALEX *makes a call on her mobile.*

KATE. In a minute it's going to ask me to match her details with the details on her photo ID. And can you call Nat?

ALEX. Don't book anything now. Hang on a minute, Kate.

KATE. Can one of you get my purse as well.

DEWI. You can't go to Australia.

KATE. Somebody has to, / somebody has to do something.

DEWI. What about Iris?

ALEX. Answerphone. Shit.

KATE. Can you get Bea's passport and my purse, please?

ALEX *calls again.*

VINNIE *enters.*

Where's Bea?

VINNIE. She's gone for a walk, can I have a bath?

KATE. What do you mean she's gone for a walk? What did you let her go out for? For Christ's sake!

VINNIE. Is she under house arrest?

KATE. See? Well done, Dewi.

DEWI. What?

KATE. Go and get her back. For God's sake.

VINNIE *exits*.

ALEX (*on phone*). Liam, it's me. Can you call me please? There's some rioting apparently in Brixton and some other places. Can you call me as soon as you get this message please because I won't be able to relax until I've spoken to you. Okay then. Definitely call me, okay? And go home. Go home now. Bye.

KATE. Right, can you call Nat now please, Alex?

ALEX. Yeah alright, Kate, sorry, I'm a bit distracted at the moment. It's a bit stressful having a teenager that's miles away and not being able to contact them while people are setting fires to cars five minutes up the road from where you've left them.

KATE. Okay, well I'm just trying to deal with the two under-fives that have been abandoned on the other side of the world at the moment.

ALEX. I know you are, and I'm with you on that. I'm just saying.

DEWI. She's going back for the boys though, isn't she?

ALEX. One minute they're tiny and tucked up in a cot upstairs and the next they're in Chicken Cottage in Peckham with a whole load of people you've never heard of.

KATE. Right. Don't touch the laptop.

ALEX. And people are setting fire to cars.

KATE *exits into the hall*.

DEWI. What's going on with Bea?

ALEX. She's upset. She's not thinking straight.

DEWI. She's going back for the boys, isn't she?

KATE *returns with her purse and* BEA*'s bag.* KATE *works on the laptop.* DEWI *hovers*.

Are you going to Melbourne?

KATE. Yes.

DEWI. How long are you going for?

KATE. I'm going with Bea to pick up the boys.

DEWI. How long for?

KATE. I don't know how long that will take, do I?

DEWI. What about Iris?

KATE. You're looking after Iris.

DEWI. How long are you going to be?

KATE. A week? I don't know, Dewi. Why? Have you got something else planned that you haven't told me about?

DEWI. No.

KATE. Because I know that we have this new rule now where we don't actually have to tell each other anything about what we're doing or thinking of doing, so technically it's none of your business how long I'm going to Melbourne for. Maybe you could just find out about my plans by overhearing one of my friends talking about them. Maybe you could just read about it in the paper. Maybe you could carry on doing your own thing and I'll carry on doing mine.

DEWI. When are you going? Are you booking a return flight?

KATE. Why don't you check the history on the laptop, you can discover all sorts of things like that, I find.

DEWI *leaves the room.*

KATE *looks over to* ALEX. ALEX *looks down at her phone.*

KATE *continues booking tickets on the laptop.*

Blackout.

Scene Three

BEA *and* VINNIE *smoking outside. It is getting dark.*

BEA. Have you got a car here, Vinnie?

VINNIE. I can use Dewi's car.

BEA. Drive me somewhere.

VINNIE. Where d'you wanna go?

BEA. To a club. Somewhere dark.

VINNIE. Now? What about supper?

BEA. After supper.

VINNIE. Kate will have something to say I reckon.

BEA. I don't want to be with people I know.

VINNIE. Right.

BEA. I don't want to talk.

VINNIE. Fair enough.

BEA. Come on, don't be so boring.

VINNIE. No, no, I'm up for it, it's cool, I'll take you wherever you want to go.

There is a pause. BEA *suddenly moves to* VINNIE *and starts to kiss him.* VINNIE *doesn't respond straight away and just as he does* BEA *moves away abruptly.*

BEA. Oh, whatever.

VINNIE. Wow. Okay!

BEA. I just want to *do* something, if I don't get out of here I'll smash my own face in.

VINNIE. It's okay, I'll take you.

BEA. Stop looking at me, just be normal –

VINNIE. I'm up for it. I haven't been clubbing for ages. Used to go down The Jack in Cardiff when Dewi was playing. The Jacquard it was called, we used to call it The Jack, 'You going down The Jack?' We'd get put straight in the VIP area at the back. We were like, Nice One! They'd all go up my mum's for breakfast as well. They never had a hotel breakfast in Cardiff. The band would go up, and whoever else was hanging around. We'd get the drivers to drop in the Tescos on the way. Loads of bangers, four packets of bacon, whatever you want, mushrooms, bish-bash, the girls on the till freaking out getting the boys to sign their autograph, they'd be getting me to sign an' all, they didn't even know who I was! I wasn't anyone!

Yeah that's it. Brilliant that was. Going down The Jack.

BEA. Can we go somewhere like that?

VINNIE. Yeah, I'll take you.

BEA. Sorry I kissed you.

VINNIE. It's cool, I just didn't know what you were doing.

BEA. I'm a bit all over the place.

Sorry.

VINNIE. No, it's good. Not like me to be so slow.

BEA. Anyway. I shouldn't have. I haven't seen you for years. Sorry.

Blackout.

Scene Four

KATE *and* BEA *are seated at the table. They have finished the meal.* VINNIE *and* ALEX *have left the table.* DEWI *is starting to clear away.*

BEA. Vinnie's going to take me into Brighton for a couple of hours, to a club or somewhere.

KATE. What?

BEA. I need to be anonymous.

KATE. Are you joking?

BEA. I really want to go. I promise we'll talk tomorrow.

KATE. What?

BEA. Please, Kate. Stop crowding me.

KATE. Stop crowding you?

BEA. I know you're trying to help me, / I appreciate that.

KATE. Crowding you? I've dropped everything, I've put everything on hold to be here for you –

BEA. I know, thanks. Just.

KATE. I'm not going to stand by / and do nothing.

BEA. I don't want to fall out with you, Kate –

KATE. While you make the worst decision of your life, / something you will regret for *ever* –

BEA. Give me some credit for having thought about this.

KATE. You want to go into Brighton to be anonymous with Vinnie? What the hell are you *doing*?

BEA. I want to be in the dark, I just need to have my ears full of sound, I need to be immersed in something.

KATE. The reason you are feeling so awful is because you are *apart* from your children, / *not* because you need to forget them.

BEA. It's not, I felt awful before, I don't want to talk about it. / Stop making me talk about it.

KATE. Something's happened that you haven't told me.

BEA. Please.

DEWI. Back off a bit, Kate.

KATE. Oh right.

DEWI. It's a bit full-on.

KATE. What? I'm the villain?

DEWI. No one's the villain.

KATE. If you turned up on my doorstep at three, four in the morning –

BEA. Ugh.

KATE. And asked me to help you, asked *anything* of me, I would be there for you. Do you know that?

BEA. If anyone was desperate enough to turn up on your doorstep at three or four in the morning, you'd be there for them. If they weren't too mentally ill. You're a kind person. You offer help and nurture to people you hardly know. That's not necessarily how friendship is defined.

KATE *goes to the door and calls:*

KATE. Alex!

KATE *returns to the table.*

BEA. Friendship is defined by what you are asking for, not what you are offering. / I think it is anyway.

KATE. Okay, so, if I went mad and separated from Iris –

BEA. If you were so unhappy –

KATE. As my friend, I would want you to do *everything* to keep us together.

BEA. Okay.

KATE. And if that meant going against my ridiculous wishes in the short term, I would want to know, absolutely, that you were looking after me in the long term, in the bigger picture.

BEA. *I* am asking you. Okay. I am asking you, my lovely
    friend, to support the decision I have made. I am asking you
    not to judge me, but to trust me. I am desperately in need of
    you to do that. Kate, please. That's all. I have weighed
    everything up, this isn't some rash, I've been thinking about
    this since Christmas, since before you and Dewi came over
    in November actually, and Kalan and Jay are so... They love
    their dad. This is my decision.

KATE. But what if I don't agree with your decision? Because,
    you know, I don't agree with your decision.

   Pause.

DEWI. Maybe you should leave it there / for the moment.

BEA. Maybe that's what friendship is. Putting that aside.
    Supporting the decision that you don't agree with. The
    decision that I have made.

KATE. How can you have decided to leave your children?

DEWI. Stop it.

KATE. No, I want to understand.

BEA. You're judging me.

KATE. You're like a robot.

BEA. I won't be judged.

KATE. You're not yourself, it's like you're hypnotised.

BEA. I am myself.

KATE. 'I won't be judged.'

   (*Calls.*) Alex!

   Anyway, it doesn't matter. Shut down, refuse to confront
   yourself, go and be 'anonymous' in some seedy club with
   Vinnie. I've bought two flights to Melbourne and we're
   going on Tuesday morning. So. That's what we're doing.

   Silence. KATE starts to clear the table.

DEWI. You've booked them?

KATE. Yep.

DEWI. Have you paid for them?

KATE. Yep.

BEA. You shouldn't have done that.

KATE. Shouldn't I? Well, I have. It's all sorted. So.

BEA. I told you I didn't want to go back.

KATE. Well, I ignored you. Because you're wrong. You are a mother.

And I feel my responsibility to your children even if you don't.

Silence.

ALEX *enters.*

ALEX. Oh my God. Guess who I've just got a text from?

KATE. Nat?

ALEX. Lewisham Council.

KATE. Saying what?

ALEX. Do you know where your child is?

KATE. What do you mean?

ALEX. It's like a ramson note.

KATE. Do you know where your child is?

ALEX. Yes. Do you know where your child is? Lewisham Council.

KATE. No, I'm asking you, do you know where your child is?

ALEX. Of course I do.

KATE. Have you spoken to him?

ALEX. No, but he'll have gone home by now, I told him to.

BEA *gets up and leaves the room.*

KATE. So you don't know where your child is.

ALEX. Yes I do. He's at home.

KATE. I thought you said he was in a chicken cottage in Peckham.

ALEX. Chicken Cottage, not a chicken cottage.

KATE. Chicken Cottage.

ALEX. It's not an actual cottage.

KATE. So he might still be there then?

ALEX. Did you think it was a cottage made of chicken in the middle of Peckham High Street? With little feather curtains.

KATE. You better ring him.

ALEX. I have rung him, his phone's off.

DEWI *is watching the riots on his phone*.

DEWI. Whoa, this is seriously kicking off.

ALEX. Let's see.

KATE. Have you rung the home phone?

ALEX. It doesn't work.

KATE. What's wrong with it?

ALEX. It does work, I just lost the handset.

KATE. You can't have lost it.

ALEX. I think I recycled it.

DEWI. Look at this, it's mad.

KATE. So you literally do not know where Liam is?

ALEX. Why are Lewisham Council texting *me*?

ALEX *takes* DEWI'*s phone*.

Oh, for fuck's sake, where's this?

DEWI. Brixton. You should probably go back to London, do you think?

KATE. What's happening?

DEWI. There are riots because of the guy the police shot / in Tottenham.

KATE. Not that, I know that. What's happening to us? Everything's falling apart.

DEWI. No it's not.

KATE. How has Bea left the boys? What is she playing at?

ALEX. Oh my God. Did you see that kid?

KATE. Everyone's slipping away. Try phoning again.

ALEX. He looks about nine.

KATE. Why didn't you just bring Liam with you? He's only fifteen.

ALEX. I didn't know this was going to happen, did I?

VINNIE *enters*.

DEWI. Maybe you should go and get him.

KATE. How can you have recycled your home phone? What kind of chaos are you living in?

ALEX. That is practically round the corner from my house. I'm not watching that.

KATE. Is it Peckham?

DEWI. It's Brixton.

ALEX. That is literally five minutes up the road from Peckham.

DEWI. Try phoning him again, Alex.

VINNIE. Where's his dad?

ALEX. Good question.

VINNIE. Can't you get his dad to go and pick him up?

ALEX. No.

KATE. She doesn't have contact with him.

VINNIE. Fair enough.

ALEX. He's in Rio anyway.

KATE. What's he doing in Rio?

ALEX. I don't know. Living there.

KATE. How do you know that? Are you in contact with him?

ALEX. No.

DEWI. Do you think you should get in the car and go and get him?

ALEX. God, do you think?

DEWI. It's a bit wild. If it was my kid.

ALEX. I don't think I can drive.

KATE. You've only had a couple of glasses of wine.

ALEX. Yes.

ALEX *looks at* VINNIE.

KATE. What?

ALEX. I had a spliff with Vinnie in the summer house. It's quite strong that stuff. I feel a bit off it. I'm not sure I should drive.

KATE. For God's sake.

ALEX. Well, I didn't think, did I?

KATE. We're supposed to be here to sort Bea out.

ALEX. I know, and I'm fine to do that.

KATE. Nice one, Vinnie.

VINNIE. I didn't start the riot.

ALEX. I just don't think I should drive.

DEWI. I'm fine to drive.

ALEX. Oh, I can't ask you to do it.

DEWI. I don't mind. Where do you think he is? At the house?

ALEX. Yes, yes, he'll be at home. He'll be in bed watching a DVD or something probably. It's just. Not being able to speak to him. I can't quite relax.

KATE. You seem quite relaxed.

ALEX. If I could just speak to him.

KATE. Getting stoned like a teenager in the 'summer house'.

ALEX. Alright, Kate.

KATE. Incredible.

BEA *enters*.

ALEX. I can't ask you to drive all the way to London, Dew, no don't.

DEWI. I don't mind.

BEA. I'll come with you.

KATE. No, no, no.

BEA. I'd like to.

KATE. Dewi likes driving on his own, don't you, Dewi.

DEWI. I don't mind. You can come if you want.

KATE. Bea, you're supposed to be here with me and Alex.

BEA. Can I come with you, Dewi?

ALEX. Oh, this is all turning into something, don't worry, Dewi.

KATE. Me and Alex have. This is special time. We have allocated this time specially.

ALEX. I feel bad about you driving all that way.

DEWI. Keep trying his phone, call me if you manage to get hold of him. I'll drive straight to the house and if he's not there I'll call you, okay?

ALEX. He will be there, he'll be in bed probably.

DEWI. And then shall I just bring him back here, yeah?

ALEX. Yeah, I'd feel better if he was here.

KATE. I don't know why you didn't just bring him in the first place.

ALEX. Thanks so much, Dewi, I really appreciate it, I'd go myself but, you know, I didn't think.

DEWI. Give me your house keys.

ALEX. I was fine before, I was like, 'Oh, he'll have gone to bed and left his phone downstairs.' Can you believe Lewisham Council sent me a text?

DEWI. It's fine. It's the right thing to do. I'll scoop him up.

DEWI *exits,* BEA *follows him.*

ALEX. I'm sorry, Kate, it's messed up your evening.

KATE. It's not my evening, it's Bea's, we're all here to concentrate on Bea.

ALEX. She doesn't want to talk to us.

KATE. For God's sake, just stop her from going with Dewi.

ALEX. Vinnie said she'd asked him to take her into Brighton.

KATE. I can't believe you got stoned with Vinnie, I wondered where you were, what's going on with you?

ALEX. Nothing. Don't make me feel bad, I didn't know I'd have to operate machinery. I'm sorry.

KATE. Just keep Bea here.

BEA *comes in with her coat on to get her bag.*

Silence.

ALEX. Don't go, Bea. It's so rare that the three of us are together. Please stay and hang out with me and Kate.

KATE. I'm sorry I got angry with you, I'm not angry with you, I'm just.

BEA. I know. It's okay.

BEA *gets a glass of water.* ALEX *motions to* KATE *to leave them on their own.* KATE *exits.*

ALEX. Come on, stay here with us.

BEA. I don't want to. I just want to go in the car with Dewi.

ALEX. You're going to come back, aren't you?

BEA. Yes.

ALEX. You're not hitching a lift back to London or anything, are you?

BEA. I'm hitching a lift into Brighton.

ALEX. What for?

BEA. I just really want to be on my own.

ALEX. Oh right. (*Pause.*) Do you want me to come with you?

BEA. No.

ALEX. Okay.

BEA. I wouldn't be on my own then, would I?

ALEX. No, I know, I just thought. (*Short laugh.*) So what, are you just going to walk by the sea and then come back?

BEA. I might.

Pause.

ALEX. Is that sensible? (*Pause.*) Okay. Well, I'm not going to interrogate you.

BEA. We'll talk tomorrow.

ALEX. Be careful though, don't wander away from the lights.

BEA. I won't.

ALEX. It's just that this was supposed to be sort of, us three talking about. Stuff. Nat as well. And, y'know, Kate's really worried about everything.

BEA. We'll talk tomorrow.

ALEX. Okay. (*Pause.*) Go on then.

BEA. See you later.

ALEX. What shall I say to Kate?

BEA *gathers her stuff.*

BEA. I'm not going back to Melbourne.

Blackout.

Scene Five

KATE, ALEX *in the sitting room.* VINNIE *smoking in the garden on the other side of the open French doors.*

ALEX. She's gone with him.

KATE. Are you joking?

ALEX. I couldn't make her stay.

KATE. Are you joking?

ALEX. No, she's gone. We can't make her speak to us.

KATE. What's she gone back to London for? She's only just got here.

ALEX. I know.

KATE. I thought she wanted to be with her friends.

ALEX. I don't know.

KATE. What is going on?

ALEX. She needs some space, I think.

KATE. Dewi'll be saying all the wrong things, just agreeing with whatever she says.

ALEX. Did you book tickets to Melbourne?

KATE. Yes I did. Tuesday 13.30 Heathrow.

ALEX. She said she's not going.

KATE. Well, she is, she has to.

Pause.

ALEX. She's terrified of something.

KATE. She just needs to get the boys back then she'll be fine.

ALEX. I know this is going to sound really unbelievably terrible and shallow, and you mustn't tell anyone I said this, ever, not ever, you have to promise –

KATE. What? Just say it.

ALEX. You know I'm not like this, don't you?

KATE. Just say the thing, what?

ALEX. I'm just going to say it really quickly and then we don't
need to speak of it again, but, if you do end up going, can
you get me some Uggs? Size six, or five and a half, if they
do half sizes.

KATE. God, Alex.

ALEX. Just, you know, if you see some, and you've got the
boys back of course. Only if everything's sorted obviously.
Don't worry about it if not. (*Pause.*) God, I feel like such a
bitch now.

KATE. It's fine, I'll get you some.

ALEX. Only, you know, just if you see some. Thanks. You
know I'm not like that, don't you, Kate? I can say it to you
because you know I'm not being, you know. They're like a
hundred and forty quid! (*Pause.*) Five and a half. Or six.

Pause.

KATE. You never told me you'd been in touch with Paddy.

ALEX. I'm not in touch with him.

KATE. You didn't tell me you contacted him.

ALEX. I know, I felt like an idiot about it. I was at a low ebb. I
heard he'd got a divorce, Liam's asthma was bad, I wrote an
email and sent it. I regretted it straight away but I couldn't
take it back.

KATE. What did he say?

ALEX. Nothing. He never even got back to me.

KATE. Bastard.

ALEX. About three weeks later I got an email from his sister
saying he'd moved to Rio. So that was that. It set me back.
It's dark on your own. I understand why Bea's scared.

KATE. But you deal with it, don't you, you can't just run away.

ALEX. I know, I'm just saying, I understand the urge to.

KATE. No you don't, you never thought like that.

ALEX. I didn't have the option, did I?

KATE. Exactly. Neither does she. None of us do. We're
    mothers.

    VINNIE *enters from the garden*.

VINNIE. What about the fathers?

KATE. God, you made me jump.

VINNIE. What's the dad like?

KATE. What are you doing? / Coming in through a door like
    that.

VINNIE. Is he alright?

KATE. Who?

VINNIE. Bea's bloke. The dad.

ALEX. I thought he was nice.

KATE. Until he stopped Bea having custody of her kids. Now,
    not so nice.

VINNIE. What's he supposed to do?

KATE. Umm, give Bea her kids back?

VINNIE. How's he supposed to do that?

KATE. Sorry, what's your point?

VINNIE. Just cos they don't get on with each other, why should
    he just fuck off out of it and let her take his kids ten thousand
    miles away?

KATE. Obviously that's not what I'm saying.

VINNIE. What are you saying then?

KATE. You've just walked in halfway through a conversation.

VINNIE. He should just give up his kids and let Bea bring them
    back to England?

KATE. Not so that he never sees them again, obviously.

VINNIE. How's he gonna see them?

KATE. Well, he'll have to work that out, won't he. I don't know. This is a whole complicated thing, you don't know the history of it. Alex, did you get to speak to Nat?

ALEX. No actually.

KATE. Can you call her I think she should come, tomorrow, don't you? It's an emergency situation. Pete's just going to have to step up for once.

VINNIE. How's he gonna see them if he's all the way over in Australia and they're here? How's he gonna do that?

KATE. He should have thought about that, shouldn't he?

VINNIE. When?

KATE. Vinnie, I don't know why you're getting so involved in this, it's nothing to do with anything, you know.

VINNIE *looks at her*.

What's your point?

VINNIE *says nothing*. ALEX *looks up*.

What's your point? Go on, say it.

VINNIE. I'm not trying to make a point. I'm just asking how it is.

KATE. I know what you're doing, okay?

VINNIE. What?

ALEX. What?

KATE. Nothing. Talking out his arse.

VINNIE. Oh yeah that's right.

KATE. As usual.

VINNIE. Yeah.

KATE. You don't know anything about Bea and what's been going on for her.

VINNIE. But this isn't really about Bea's kids, is it? / Why can't you just be honest with yourself?

KATE. No, I don't care about them. / Shut up, Vinnie.

VINNIE. Just trying to keep everyone in their place, isn't it?

KATE. Yeah, because I don't care about my four-year-old godson actually, Kalan's my godson you know.

VINNIE. Yeah I know that.

KATE. And Jay's your godson isn't he, Alex? / His little two-year-old brother.

ALEX. No, he's Nat's. Connie's mine.

KATE. So, you know. We have responsibilities.

VINNIE. Yeah? That's interesting.

KATE. Something you don't have a massive amount of experience of, so, / you know. Thanks for the input.

VINNIE. My God, you are unbelievable.

KATE. And can you keep your voice down, please, I don't want Iris getting woken up / by your big booming stoned voice.

VINNIE. Whatever.

KATE. Oh, very grown up. (*Pause.*) I am absolutely not prepared. To get in to. I know what you're alluding to, you're desperate to bring it up, / I knew you had this up your sleeve.

VINNIE. Doesn't fit in, does it.

KATE. No, it's just not something I wish to discuss *now*. / Or with you.

VINNIE. Fine. Fine.

KATE. Looking for a fight.

VINNIE. I'm not looking for a fight, it's a genuine question, right, all I'm saying is.

KATE. Here it comes –

VINNIE. What about Dewi's responsibility? What about Dewi's responsibility to his first daughter, his other daughter? What about that? Not his goddaughter or his friend's daughter.

Silence. KATE *looks at* ALEX.

ALEX. I don't think we should talk about this either, Vinnie. You know. And Dewi's not here, to defend himself.

VINNIE. Defend himself against what?

KATE. Oh yes, because it was all *my* fault, wasn't it, Vinnie? She means, give his side of the story.

VINNIE. He doesn't have a side of the story, though, does he? That is exactly the point. There is no story for him, is there? He's not even allowed that, is he?

KATE. Because Dewi's totally blameless, isn't he? Yeah.

VINNIE. No one's allowed to talk about it. It didn't happen. Nothing happened. That's right, isn't it? Fine. I'm under your roof. I won't say another word.

Pause. No one looks at one another.

KATE *eventually stands.*

KATE. Do you want anything, Alex? Can I get anyone…?

ALEX. No, I'm fine thanks. I think I'll just. Maybe I should try Liam again. Leave a message at least. About Dewi on his way.

KATE. Yes. That's a good idea.

ALEX. He'll be asleep I expect.

KATE. Oh yes, he'll be fine. Safe and sound tucked up in bed.

ALEX. Aaah, I know.

KATE. Little Liam.

ALEX. I know.

Pause.

KATE. Sure you don't want a cup of anything?

ALEX. Are you having one?

KATE. I might have a peppermint tea.

ALEX. Yes, I will as well then.

KATE. Vinnie?

VINNIE. No thanks.

KATE. Do you want a builder's tea?

VINNIE. No thanks.

Pause.

Then KATE *exits.*

ALEX *makes a call.* VINNIE *watches her.*

When she leaves a message she is a little self-conscious.

ALEX. Hi, Liam, it's Mum. Dewi's driving over to the house to pick you up. I can't relax here with you there. There's still some rioting and it's quite nearby. Not that nearby. I should have brought you with me. So can you get ready and come back with him? He's driven all the way over there so make sure you are very friendly and chatty. Don't fall asleep in the car. Tell him about the thing you were doing in civilisation about the illegal immigrants. Tell him about your band. And make sure you double lock the door and leave the hall light on. Actually call me when you get this. Anyway. Bye, bye, bye, don't leave the house till Dewi gets there, bye.

ALEX *hangs up.* ALEX *looks at* VINNIE.

I think that gear's made me paranoid, he'll be fine, won't he? Ridiculous, Dewi driving all the way over there. Sirens blaring. What an overreaction.

VINNIE. Fuck it. You lot really piss me off, do you know that? Why can't anyone ever bring this up?

ALEX. Jesus, Vinnie, it's obviously not the time.

VINNIE. When is the time then? She'll be fourteen in October. Next minute she'll be sixteen and then 'ding dong', on the doorstep. How's Kate going to deal with her then. 'Sorry, you do not exist in my version of events. Please get the next train home.'

ALEX. That won't happen, will it? How's she going to know the address?

VINNIE. Are you for real?

ALEX. It was years ago, they've moved about five times since then. The chances are she'll have another dad anyway.

VINNIE. Yeah cos it's not as if Dewi's traceable, is it? They haven't invented the internet, have they? No one's ever heard of him, he can just disappear off the edge of the earth. You're as bad as her.

ALEX. I just think it's unlikely, that all of a sudden. If they wanted to trace him they'd have done it by now.

VINNIE. You lot have no idea.

ALEX. Why do you have to bring it up now?

VINNIE. She's a person, she's a young woman. You lot think, oh that messy little mistake Dewi made all them years ago, if we don't ever think about it it won't have happened.

ALEX. Do you know her?

VINNIE. We'll just carry on, course I bloody know her, she lives in Cathays, doesn't she, everyone knows her.

ALEX. God. Does Kate know that?

VINNIE. Everyone knows everyone, don't they?

ALEX. Does Dewi know?

VINNIE. Know what?

ALEX. That you know where the baby is.

VINNIE. What baby, she's not a baby, she's fourteen. Time doesn't stand still cos you've looked away. She's a bright and funny and caring young woman, she's clever, she's in all the top groups, the gifted and talented groups, she came second in the Eisteddfod last year, she did her poem in the Millenium Centre, in front of thousands it was. She's, she's fucking great.

ALEX. Oh right. I didn't know.

VINNIE. Dewi knows. Of course Dewi knows. He's not
allowed to know, though, is he? He's not fucking allowed to
know anything that doesn't comply with orders, is he?

ALEX. It was terrible for Kate, that time, she was almost
destroyed by his, that was a massive betrayal of trust, Vinnie.
No wonder she couldn't be generous, she *forgave* him, oh
my God, that is not easy to do, she forgave him, she took
him back, she rebuilt the relationship. If it wasn't for her,
her. Strength and courage, God knows.

KATE *enters with two cups of tea.*

Ooh lovely, thank you, Kate.

KATE. Did you speak to Liam?

ALEX. No, I left a message though. He'll be fine. I'm
embarrassed now, letting Dewi go.

KATE. Yeah well, it's done now. (*Pause.*) If you don't mind,
Vinnie, Alex and I need to get on with some planning. We
need to talk. Privately.

VINNIE. All I'm saying is, y'know, Bea's ex. Cut the guy some
slack, c'mon. He sounds like a decent bloke.

KATE. Me and Alex need to get on with stuff.

VINNIE. For fuck's sake, why do you even need to get involved?
Just let them work it out for themselves. Maybe they *are* better
off with him. Bea's not exactly bothered, is she?

KATE. Thank you, Vinnie.

VINNIE. Well, she's not, is she? Fucking off into Brighton,
hanging out with teenagers in a club.

KATE. She's gone to collect Liam with Dewi actually.

ALEX. No, she has gone into Brighton.

KATE. I thought she'd gone with Dewi.

ALEX. She was going to get out in Brighton.

KATE. He won't drive through Brighton, he doesn't go that
way. I'm going to ring him. Why didn't you say that before?

VINNIE. Quick, give him a ring. He might have a thought you haven't vetoed.

KATE. Do you know what, if you hate me that much, Vinnie –

VINNIE. He might actually have an opinion all of his own –

KATE. Then can I suggest you go back to your own house –

VINNIE. He might suddenly realise he's been led by you for so long he hasn't got a clue who he is, or where the fuck he's going.

KATE. Oh no sorry, you don't have a house of your own, do you? You're still staying with your mum, aren't you, / or with whatever lucky lady is the current.

VINNIE. And why don't I have my own house, yeah? / What do you think I've been doing with every bit of cash.

KATE. Oh okay, let's go the whole hog. Go on. Why don't you have your own house, Vinnie?

VINNIE. Every bit of cash I've had I've given to Leanne and Sue.

KATE. Have you? Oh right, good for you. / Well done.

ALEX. Who are Leanne and Sue?

KATE. He is talking utter bollocks.

VINNIE. Every penny I gave to that girl. Fucking, on her own with a kid, *nothing* she got from Dewi, *nothing* – / Okay, listen to this right. Do you *know* how ashamed my family were? Oh my God you have *no idea* –

KATE. It was her decision. / All or nothing she said –

ALEX. You've been giving money to the girl that Dewi slept with?

KATE. No he hasn't, / of course he hasn't.

VINNIE. I've done what I can / because *she* wouldn't even let Dewi *talk* about it.

KATE. Sorry, sorry, can we at least. He hasn't been giving anyone any money, okay? / It's fictional.

VINNIE. She, categorically, right. She...

KATE. Ooh, tripped up on the long word there –

VINNIE. Never let Dewi mention it again and he was so
     ashamed, right, / that he did everything he could for her
     forgiveness –

KATE. Can we at least get the *facts* straight here if we have to
     bring this stupid matter up, / dragging it kicking and
     screaming back up from the fucking *past* –

ALEX. I thought Dewi just accidentally had a bit of a shag with
     a groupie, I didn't know she was still *around*. / I didn't know
     anyone *knew* her –

VINNIE. Where did you think she had gone? She grew up!
     She's, she's fucking beautiful, she is. Iris is the spit of her.

KATE. No, no, no, right! (*Stands.*)

VINNIE. She fucking *is*, man.

KATE. That is enough. Stop right there.

VINNIE. Dewi was so eaten up about it, he just did everything
     you said, everything to stop you from leaving him. He gave
     everything up. The band, music, his writing, the *family*,
     listening to anyone other than you, he gave up his moral
     responsibility, his instinct, his honour. You stripped him of, he
     was a *slave* to winning back your trust. What about Leanne?
     She's nearly fourteen. How's she going to trust anyone?

ALEX. What, and you've been supporting her?

KATE. Of course he hasn't. It's a fantasy, he's never *earnt*
     anything for a start –

VINNIE. Oh my God, you are toxic, you, we've all had to
     pussyfoot around you, 'don't mention it, don't mention it',
     my mother's been too scared to have a granddaughter in case
     Dewi gets into trouble over it. She bought a Boots token,
     right, just a tenner, you know, on a gift-card thing, I was like,
     'Who's the token for?' She starts crying. 'It's Leanne's
     thirteenth birthday,' she goes, 'I was going to send it
     anonymously.' Fucking hell. Send it anonymously? A

fucking anonymous nana? What's that all about? Oh my God, the *control* you have over us.

KATE. Right, for a start, I have never. I have never said your mother can't do what the hell she likes in regards to –

VINNIE. How can she be a nana if Dewi isn't allowed to be a dad? She's Dewi's mum, how's that going to work?

KATE. Well, that's between her and Dewi –

VINNIE. She knows it would break Dewi's heart, / he's *buried* it. He's had to.

KATE. What? What would it break his heart for?

VINNIE. It killed him, having to turn his back.

KATE. Oh right. I'm sorry. Let's not fabricate a whole Channel 4 drama.

ALEX. Did Dewi want to have a role in the baby's life?

KATE. Of course he didn't –

VINNIE. Of course he wanted to, he wanted to but *you* wouldn't have it –

KATE. You know absolutely nothing of what went on with me and Dewi. / How dare you say that.

VINNIE. He did what you told him he had to do to get everything back to normal, you know he did.

KATE. The girl said all or nothing, she didn't want Dewi to play a minor role, happy families or fuck off, and he wasn't going to play happy families with her, was he? It was her choice. She didn't have to even have the baby, did she? It was her choice.

ALEX. I thought / it was one of those out-of-control, off-your-head moments with a groupie.

VINNIE. She didn't *have* a choice! You forced him into a corner, you made him turn his back. She wasn't a fucking groupie, it was Sue, it's Sue, she was the PR, one of the PR girls, she was *on* the tour, she was at school with Gary's brother. / It's Sue!

KATE. I can't have this conversation any more –

VINNIE. Dewi would have loved to support her, he was earning shedloads of money, it was completely against his nature, he went against every instinct he had. For you. And he has *never* recovered from that.

KATE. So how is that my fault? I refuse. Sorry. I do not have to discuss any of this stuff with you.

Pause.

VINNIE. You let him do that for you. It was wrong. You should of encouraged him / to play his part.

KATE. I thought you had a problem with me telling him what to do. And now it's a problem I let him do what he wanted to do. Fuck *off*, Vinnie. I'm already in turmoil about Bea and the boys in Melbourne, I don't have the head space, I don't have the *strength* for this. (*Pause*.) A baby needs to be with the mother, Alex, you know that, look at Alex! Three kids, three fathers, and where are they? Argentina!

ALEX. Brazil.

KATE. Brazil! Don't listen to him, he's making a whole load of stuff up to make himself significant.

ALEX. But, God. Vinnie, that's amazing that you've been supporting her.

KATE. Alex, hello, he's talking total nonsense. You were in prison for half her life anyway, how did you manage to support her from there? / How *did* they manage to survive without you?

VINNIE. Ten months, I was in prison for ten months.

KATE. You didn't support anything, it takes more than popping round occasionally to bring up a child.

VINNIE. I'm not going to justify myself to you, I supported them. I helped them when I could. I paid for things, I saw them right. Leanne's my niece.

KATE. Well, judging by your input up to now in Iris's life I don't imagine your role as Uncle Vinnie cost you that much.

You know, the pink Converse were sweet. But, they don't really wear shoes when all they do is lie down, so, bit useless.

ALEX. Kate.

KATE. What?

ALEX. Stop it.

KATE. What?

ALEX. You've got to come back from this, remember.

KATE. What?

ALEX. He's Dewi's brother.

Silence.

Blackout.

Scene Six

Sitting room. 2.30 a.m.

A car pulls up outside, engine running, car door closes, front door.

BEA *enters and switches on a light. She scans the room and sees* ALEX's *handbag. She finds her purse. She looks inside and finds notes. She runs out the room with the money.*

LIAM *sits up from his position under a duvet on the sofa. He listens. The car engine starts to drive away. The front door closes and he lies back down.* BEA *enters. She goes straight to the laptop. She still has her coat on. After a moment, the Skype call tone can be heard. Four or five rings.*

A woman picks up.

WOMAN'S VOICE. Hello? Hello?

BEA. Dana? It's Bea. / Are the boys there?

WOMAN'S VOICE. Bea? Are you okay? / Where are you?

BEA. I'm good, Dana, I'm fine, are the boys there?

WOMAN'S VOICE. Kalan's at nursery, I'm going to get him at twelve, / where are you?

BEA. Oh, what time is it? / I thought –

WOMAN'S VOICE. Eleven thirty. Jay's having his nap, shall I wake him?

BEA. No, don't wake him, / I've done the maths wrong, is it nine hours? Don't worry.

WOMAN'S VOICE. I have to wake him in a minute anyway. Are you in England? Where are you, Bea? What's happening? / Simon said you'd gone back to England.

BEA. I'll call again, when you've got Kalan from nursery. Don't worry.

WOMAN'S VOICE. Is everything okay? When are you coming home?

BEA. Are they...? Has Kalan...? I'll call later, Dana.

WOMAN'S VOICE. Put the camera on, hang on, I can hear Jay, he's stirring. / Wait.

BEA. I'll call later, it's okay. Sorry, sorry, I have to go.

WOMAN'S VOICE. Wait!

    BEA *closes the laptop and puts it away from her.*

    LIAM *sits up.*

LIAM. Hey.

BEA. Oh my God!

LIAM. Hi.

BEA. God, sorry, I didn't realise you were there. / Hey. Hi.

LIAM. I was just lying here / listening to the radio.

BEA. I didn't realise, of course, Dewi went to get you, how was it? Were you okay? With the rioting.

LIAM. It was mad. Yeah.

BEA. Okay. So you were okay? Not caught up in / anything scary.

LIAM. It was crazy. A boy in my year got arrested for like, wearing a hat. The police are off their heads.

BEA. Shit.

LIAM. Yeah.

BEA. God, Liam, I can't believe, you look so, grown up.

LIAM. Yeah well I'm fifteen, so.

BEA. I know! Wow!

LIAM. Yeah.

Pause.

BEA. So, I'm just. I've just been out. I just got back.

LIAM. Do you know how to turn the camera on? On the Skype?

BEA. Yeah, yeah. No, it's fine, I'm going to call back later on. That's all cool. So, how are you?

LIAM. Yeah. Cool.

BEA. Yeah? That's great.

Pause.

LIAM. How come you're here?

BEA. Umm.

LIAM. How come you've left Kalan and Jay behind?

BEA. I haven't left them behind.

LIAM. Oh. So where are they?

BEA. With their dad, so, yeah.

LIAM. Okay. (*Pause.*) Do you want me to show you how to turn the camera on?

BEA. I know how to do it, Liam. Thanks.

*BEA takes off her coat. She has big red marks down the
backs of her arms.*

LIAM. What's that on your arm?

BEA. Where?

LIAM. On the back of your arm, there. It's scraped.

BEA. I think I scraped it on a wall.

LIAM. There's blood on it.

BEA. I sort of fell into a wall.

Pause.

LIAM. Are you drunk?

BEA. Yes. I possibly am slightly. Sorry about that!

LIAM. I don't care. I've seen my mum drunk loads of times.
She's always drunk. She drinks a bottle of wine practically
every night –

BEA. Not every night.

LIAM. She does. And in the morning she's like, 'Oh darling,
can you get some ibuprofen?' She's drunk now. That's why
Dewi came to get me. She was too drunk. She'd been calling
my old mobile number, I haven't had it for about three
months. She keeps doing that. I sold my old number to my
mate, right, because he was like blacklisted. And she sends
him texts and everything. He's like, 'I got a text from your
mum.' I'm like, 'Man, why does she keep that old number in
her phone?' She doesn't even know how to delete it. She
spent about half an hour putting in Liam Old Mobile, and
Liam New Mobile, I go, 'What did you do that for? Just
delete it, it'll take like half a second.' She's going. 'Aaaah,
that was your first mobile number, I can't delete it out, it's so
sweet.' Oh my days. I swear to God. She sent me a text once,
it just said Thk, or like, Twk? I'm like, what the fuck? She is
such a drunk, I am not joking.

BEA (*laughing*). Has she gone to bed?

LIAM. She's with Dewi's brother in the summer house. She
pretended to go to bed but she sneaked out there. They're

getting stoned. I bet you, in the morning, she'll be like, 'Can you get me some ibuprofen?'

BEA. Oh, Liam, you're so funny.

LIAM. Seriously. I'm like, grow up.

BEA. Aaah, she's a great mother, though, isn't she?

LIAM. She's alright.

BEA. The three of you boys, all by herself. She's done so well. (*Pause.*) Hasn't she?

LIAM. Yeah, I suppose.

BEA. Well, I think she has. Credit where credit's due.

Silence.

BEA *suddenly reaches for* LIAM*'s hand.*

I feel so lost, Liam.

Silence. LIAM *looks away.*

Sorry, you don't want to know that.

Silence.

LIAM *scrolls through his iPod.*

I remember you when you were a baby! I watched you get your nappy changed! Oh my God, can you believe that? Look at you! You're so big! You're like a man.

LIAM. How old are Kalan and Jay now?

BEA. Oh, Liam, you're a man! How can that be? Will you drink something with me? Don't tell anyone, I won't tell anyone, come on, let's see what we can find.

BEA *gets up and goes into the kitchen.* LIAM *stands and goes to the French doors, he looks out into the night. He opens the doors.*

LIAM (*softly calls*). Mum! (*Pause.*) Mum!

For fuck's sake.

LIAM *closes the doors and comes back to the sofa.*

BEA *enters with a bottle of wine and a corkscrew.*

BEA. I can't open it, I can't do it.

BEA *hands him the bottle.*

LIAM. It's a screw-top.

LIAM *opens the bottle.* BEA *gets her glass.*

BEA. You're so clever. You can share this glass with me.

LIAM. No, you're alright.

BEA. I want to share it with you, Liam, come on. Don't abandon me.

The Skype tone sounds. BEA *freezes.*

LIAM. Hey, they're calling you back.

BEA. Oh!

LIAM. Shall I get it?

BEA. No, no.

LIAM. Do you know how to do it?

BEA. Yes, I know how to. I'm just. Not. I don't feel like talking at the moment.

The Skype tone continues. BEA *doesn't move.*

LIAM. Aren't you going to answer it though?

The tone continues for a long time. BEA *doesn't move.*

What if it's Kalan?

BEA *doesn't move.*

Aren't you going to?

Skype tone stops.

BEA *doesn't look at* LIAM. *After a moment he stands up and goes to the French doors and looks out. After a while.*

BEA. Can I ask you something, Liam?

LIAM. What?

BEA. You don't have to answer me. If it's private, that's fine.

LIAM. What?

BEA. Do you feel damaged? –

LIAM. No.

BEA. No, I mean, do you feel emotionally, do you feel that your choices in life, do you feel, you know, fucked up? By, what happened to you. You know, your dad and all that.

LIAM. No.

Pause.

BEA. Oh well, that's great. (*Pause.*) So you don't feel full of rage, or you know, unhappy? Because your dad. Bowed out.

LIAM. Bowed out?

BEA. Stepped away. Chose not to. Be an active part of your daily life.

LIAM. No.

BEA. Okay, that's great. (*Pause.*) And. Do you ever think about your dad?

LIAM. Sometimes. Not really.

Pause.

BEA. And, you know, when you do. If you ever do. You don't have to answer this, by the way. But, when you do think about him, on the rare, you know. What do you think?

LIAM. I dunno really.

Pause.

BEA. That's okay. You don't have to say.

LIAM. Sometimes, I think, like, you know when something happens to you and like it happens to your mate at the same time? You know like if you get a text message at exactly the same time that your mate's phone gets a text. And your phone's like, beep beep, and his phone's like, beep beep, at the exact same time and you're like, oh my God, that's such a coincidence? Or like you both go into a shop and you get split up but when you come out you've got like the exact same stuff? The same drink, or whatever.

BEA. Right.

LIAM. Sometimes I think that. You know. That's weird but what about all the times when that happens but you *don't even know*. How weird is *that*? Like sometimes if I'm like biting into a sandwich or whatever, and I think, what if, you know, my dad was like biting into a sandwich at like, the exact same time? Or like, the same kind of sandwich? Or like when I put the TV on standby before I go to bed and the house is really quiet and then I think, you know, as I take like a step or move my hand to like, pick up my glass, wouldn't it be weird if like, me and my dad were moving at exactly the same time, at the same speed, like synchronised swimmers but not even knowing. Sometimes I think that.

Pause.

BEA. That is so beautiful.

Pause.

LIAM. And other times I think, you know, what a cunt!

BEA. Oh!

LIAM. But mostly, I don't think about him at all.

BEA. Yes, that's. Normal reaction. (*Pause.*) Sorry to ask you all that. Thanks for being honest.

LIAM. No worries.

BEA. It's just. I don't know. I just feel so lost.

Pause. LIAM *returns to the sofa and sits.*

LIAM. I know what to do about that.

BEA. Do you?

LIAM. From a camp I went on, with the Outward Bound Trust. I went with my friend and his dad. It was the best ten days of my entire life.

BEA. Wow. Sounds amazing.

LIAM. So, like if you were lost in a wood. Or the desert.

BEA. I'm not really that kind of lost.

LIAM. What kind of lost are you?

BEA. It doesn't matter. Sorry, Liam, what a drag. I'll work it out.

LIAM. We went on this like, Ultimate-Adventure thing. We had to camp out in the middle of like nowhere, with like, nothing. I got like ticks, in my leg, that were this big! You have to pinch them and twist them out so you don't pull their body off and leave the rest of them inside you. They teach you how to make a shelter sort of thing, and how to light a fire and get clean water and not die, basically. Like serious survival techniques.

BEA. Amazing! Where were you?

LIAM. The Lake District. It was seriously cool. My mate's dad, he was seriously cool, he like used to be a proper explorer when he was young and went on like major expeditions and stuff. He went to like Canada and shit.

BEA. Okay. So. I'm lost. On my own, in a dark, creepy wood.

LIAM. Okay. Have you got a compass?

BEA. No compass.

LIAM. Have you got a map?

BEA. No.

LIAM. Okay. Like, is anyone going to come looking for you if you're not back by nightfall sort of thing?

BEA. No. No one knows I'm there.

LIAM. Okay. Well, you're a bit of an idiot, no disrespect. You're supposed to like tell people, what you're doing and like be prepared and stuff.

BEA. Okay. Well, I haven't done that.

LIAM. Have you got like water and supplies?

BEA. Nothing. I am the most idiot it is possible to be.

LIAM. Okay.

BEA. Go on then. Tell me how to get out of here, I'm lost, Liam, it's half two in the morning, get on with it.

LIAM. Okay. Well, the first thing you have to do is stay where you are. Right, so like, loads of people would think you have to try to find a way out by like walking to different places, but that's wrong. You have to think about, that if the like, search party, are going to find you, you have to work, like, with them. The more you move about the more difficult it is for you to be found, right. You are always just one person, in one place, and if you move somewhere else, to get firewood or find a clean water source or whatever, you have to leave signs. Like twigs that spell out SOS. Or arrows to your camp, or like a triangle in the earth, because that's like an international distress signal. And like, even in the summer, it can get like mega-cold at night. Hypothermia is like, your biggest enemy, and so you have to wear all your clothes and even like cut a hole in your bag and pull that over your head. So you keep warm until they find you.

BEA. Okay.

LIAM. Yeah.

BEA. But I haven't told anyone that I'm there, so no one knows I'm likely to be lost, remember. So there won't be any search party looking for me, will there?

LIAM. Yeah, but.

BEA. No one to see my international distress signal. Or find me with my bag on my head.

LIAM. Not *on* your head. Over your head, like a jumper.

BEA. No one's looking for me, Liam. I'm more lost than that.

LIAM. Have you got a phone?

BEA. No phone.

LIAM. Okay. You need to build a fire. Then you've got a smoke signal, and it keeps you warm. So you have to like, get some paper –

BEA. Er?

LIAM. Okay, some small dry twigs, and anything like green. Green leaves make like a really thick smoke. So you light the fire.

BEA. With?

LIAM. Like a match.

BEA. No matches.

LIAM. What have you got?

BEA. Nothing.

LIAM. Okay.

BEA. I told you, I'm totally ill-equipped.

LIAM. Right. (*Pause.*) No offence right. But you'll probably, like, die.

BEA. In the Lake District?

LIAM. Well. No.

    BEA *laughs*.

    Not in the Lakes, because there's like loads of people doing like Ultimate Adventure and stuff, but if you were on a proper expedition, like Fergus's dad.

BEA. Is that it? Is that all you can do for me? All your stuff's just about not doing anything. Waiting to be rescued.

LIAM. You're more likely to survive if you stay put. Discomfort is not a reason not to stay where you are, they said. You can survive three times longer than you think you can, Fergus's dad said. So stay put, yeah. Unless there's like an avalanche, when you know, you should probably move. That's just common sense.

    ALEX *enters from the garden. She is sheepish. She is dressed but a bit dishevelled.*

ALEX. Bea!

BEA. Hi, Alex.

ALEX. Liam, did you call me?

LIAM. Ages ago, yeah.

ALEX. Sorry, darling, I wasn't sure if it was you.

LIAM. Who did you think it was?

ALEX. Are you okay? Did you need me?

LIAM. No, it doesn't matter now.

ALEX. Okay. (*Pause.*) Hello, Bea.

BEA. Hi.

ALEX. Are you okay? Is everything?

BEA. Yes.

ALEX. Thanks for your text. I was starting to get worried.

BEA. Yeah, sorry. I met some people. We just sort of, hung out.

ALEX. Oh, right. And are you feeling?

BEA. Yeah. A bit.

ALEX. Okay, well, we'll talk in the morning, won't we? I might go for a run. I probably won't.

LIAM. I need to be back in London for eight tomorrow.

ALEX. Eight in the morning? Oh God. Do you?

LIAM. Can you drive me?

ALEX. Not for eight! Does it matter? Is it for something important?

LIAM. Yeah. Oboe.

ALEX. Oh God, can't you miss it? Bea's having a tricky. Are you okay, Bea? Sorry about.

BEA. Liam's just telling me all about everything.

ALEX. About Dewi practically breaking down our front door?

BEA. No, what's that?

ALEX. I gave Dewi the wrong keys! They were my work keys! Liam was fast asleep in bed, he wasn't out rioting at all!

Lewisham bloody Council nearly giving me a heart attack. It was all fine round our area. It was older boys that were the problem, Dewi said. Other people's kids, thank you, Lewisham.

BEA. Liam was telling me all about his camping trip.

ALEX. Oh God, were you being forced to listen? What camping?

LIAM. With Fergus's dad.

ALEX. Oh God, that was ages ago.

LIAM. No it wasn't. I thought you went to bed anyway.

ALEX. Bea, listen. I'm going to get up bright and early and we can have a proper breakfast together and. Kate's up early with Iris, so the three of us can sort everything out then.

BEA. I'll come out actually. I'll have a cigarette before I go to bed.

ALEX. Oh yes, come out.

BEA. Liam, thank you so much for chatting to me. I can't believe Liam's fifteen!

ALEX. I know, it's ridiculous.

BEA. We've had such a lovely chat.

ALEX. Oh well, that's a miracle. He won't chat to me. I'd love you to chat to me!

LIAM. Shut up.

ALEX. Night night, sweetheart. Give us a kiss.

LIAM *kisses her.*

Love you. (*Laughing.*) 'Shut up, Mum, you're so embarrassing.'

BEA *and* ALEX *exit into the garden.*

LIAM *is left alone on the sofa.*

He sits still. After a moment he starts to move really slowly. His hand, as if under water, to the glass on the table, then slow lift of the glass to his lips. He stands, steps, turns, dance-like, in slow motion.

The Skype tone sounds.

LIAM *goes straight to the computer. He answers the call.*

LIAM. Hello. Hello.

MAN'S VOICE (*children loud in background*). Hello. Dewi?

LIAM. No, it's Liam, Alex's son.

MAN'S VOICE. Hi, Liam, it's Simon. Bea's... Hi.

LIAM. Hello.

CHILD'S VOICE. Mummy! Where's Mummy? I can't see her!

SIMON'S VOICE. Is Bea there with you, Liam?

LIAM *turns on the camera. The faces light up on the screen. There is* KALAN (*four years old*) *and in the background* JAY (*eighteen months*) *not looking at the camera.* LIAM*'s face can be seen in the corner of the screen.*

LIAM. She's just stepped out. Hang on. I'll run and.

KALAN. I can't see her!

SIMON'S VOICE. Thanks, Liam. Hey, it's the middle of the night with you guys, did I wake you? Dana, our nanny called me, she said Bea had just called here, I reckoned she'd be awake.

LIAM. She is, it's cool. Hang on, I'll get her.

VINNIE *is standing at the French doors watching the call.* LIAM *turns to him.*

Is Bea? Is my mum?

VINNIE. I'll find her.

VINNIE *goes.*

LIAM. She won't be a minute. Dewi's brother has just gone to get her.

SIMON'S VOICE. Thanks, Liam.

Silence for a few moments. Then:

LIAM. Hi, Kalan.

SIMON. Say hi! You remember Liam, don't you? Liam came to visit you at Granny's, with Benji and Hal.

KALAN (*to* SIMON). Where's Mummy?

LIAM. Hey, Kalan. You still playing swingball?

SIMON. Hey yeah, you remember playing swingball with Liam, don't you, Kalan? Do you still play swingball, he's asking you.

LIAM. I played swingball with you, Kalan, and you were really good at it.

SIMON. Yeah, you love your swingball, don't you, Kalan?

LIAM. Your mum won't be a minute, Kalan.

LIAM turns to look at the door, as VINNIE *returns.*

VINNIE. She won't come.

LIAM. What? / Why not?

VINNIE. She won't come.

KALAN's face looms large on the screen.

LIAM (*to* VINNIE, *off-camera*). It's Kalan though.

VINNIE. I know. I said the kids are waiting to speak to her, but she says she can't come.

LIAM. One minute, Kalan.

LIAM moves aside and gives VINNIE *the computer.*
VINNIE's face appears in the corner of the screen. LIAM *exits into the garden.*

VINNIE. Alright, Kalan, I'm Vinnie.

KALAN moves back. SIMON *comes into the picture.*

He is the man from the hotel room.

He stands looking into the camera. He moves KALAN *to the side.*

SIMON. One minute, Kalan.

What's going on? Is Bea coming or what?

VINNIE. I think so. I'm not sure what's going on.

SIMON. This is cruel, you know. She called here. What's she playing at? I need to speak to her, please.

VINNIE. I know. Liam's gone to see.

There is a commotion outside.

LIAM *and* ALEX *can be seen through the door.*

LIAM. What the fuck? Kalan's like, waiting to speak to her.

ALEX. What on earth are you thinking of? You cannot speak to Bea like that. / You have no idea what's going on for her.

VINNIE. I think, I think she's just stepped out for a moment. Maybe if she like, calls you back?

SIMON. Can I just speak to Bea, please?

LIAM. Kalan's waiting. Fucking! He's asking for her.

ALEX. How dare you speak to Bea like that, how dare you put your hands! / Stop swearing at me.

LIAM. How dare she not come? How dare she not, like speak to her child?

ALEX. This is none of your. Stop shouting! You have no idea what's going on. / You can't just start screaming at Bea, oh my God!

LIAM. Fuck off. I know what's going on! I'm not a kid! I can see what's going on. Fuck off!

KALAN *pushes his face back in front of the camera.*

KALAN. Boo!

VINNIE. Aaargh! What's that? Is it a monster?

KALAN *laughs, he makes monster faces.*

You're scary!

ALEX. You are totally out of order. Will you stop shouting, Liam. / It's three o'clock in the morning. Iris is asleep.

LIAM. Fuck off. You're off your head.

ALEX. Right. That's enough. / Apologise to Bea now.

LIAM. Make her come. Make her speak to Kalan.

ALEX. Stop shouting. / You can't make people do things, Liam.

LIAM. She's a fucking freak!

ALEX. Stop shouting.

LIAM. What the fuck is wrong with her?

KATE enters the sitting room. She looks at KALAN's face on the screen. She looks at LIAM in the garden.

VINNIE (*to* KALAN). What's the scariest face you can make?

KATE. For God's sake. End the call, Vinnie.

KALAN makes a scarier face.

VINNIE. Aaargh! That's scary!

KATE. End the call.

On the screen DANA puts a plate of lunch down in front of KALAN. He eats.

VINNIE watches him.

ALEX. Come inside, Liam, oh my God, look, you've woken up Kate and Dewi now.

LIAM is pushing ALEX away.

LIAM. I don't care. You can all fuck off. Why did you make me come here? Fucking freaks. I didn't want to be here anyway.

LIAM starts to walk away. ALEX is holding on to him. He breaks free after a scuffle.

ALEX. Liam!

LIAM. Get the fuck off me, I fucking hate you.

ALEX speaks into the room. DEWI has come into the room too.

ALEX. I am so sorry about my son. I am so sorry, Kate. Sorry, Dewi. Oh my God. I am mortified.

KATE. Where's Bea?

ALEX. I don't know. Liam screamed at her, he tried to put his hands on her neck! She ran off. Oh my God! This. Is why I didn't bring him with me.

KATE. Dewi, go and find Bea.

DEWI. I'm going to speak to Liam first.

KATE. No, find Bea. / She's lost out there.

DEWI. Don't tell me what to do.

ALEX. Yes, can you go after him, Dewi. Please. I don't know what's wrong with him!

DEWI *exits*.

Thank you so much, Dewi, thank you. Sorry! Oh my God. He totally lost it with Bea. I have never seen him like this.

KALAN*'s face is on the screen looking out. He does a scary face.*

VINNIE. Wow! That is the scariest face I've ever seen!

KATE. End the call, Vinnie.

ALEX. My legs are shaking. Oh dear, this is such a mess.

On the screen. KALAN*'s scary face.*

KALAN *roars*.

BEA *runs in from the garden*.

Bea! I am so, so sorry about Liam. Bea.

BEA *goes up to* VINNIE, *she takes the laptop and slams down the lid.*

The screen goes blank.

VINNIE. Whooooa!

LIAM *comes into the doorway.* DEWI *following*.

LIAM. What did you do that for?

ALEX. That's enough. I am so sorry, Bea. Are you alright?

LIAM. Kalan wanted to speak to you, he wanted to see you. He just wanted to hear your voice.

KATE. It's the middle of the night –

LIAM. Why won't you speak to him? What has he done wrong?

DEWI. Nothing.

ALEX. Stop it, Liam, leave her alone.

LIAM. Why isn't she answering me?

DEWI. He hasn't done anything wrong.

LIAM. Why have you brought me here? It's all fucked, / I don't want to be here.

ALEX. Can you apologise to Bea, please, Liam.

LIAM. What?

DEWI. It's alright, Alex, just leave it. / Bea understands, don't you, Bea?

LIAM. Why do I have to apologise to her? What have I done?

DEWI. You haven't done anything.

ALEX. You shouted in her face, you put your hands on her neck, / you rushed into a situation, you don't know anything about it.

LIAM. She wouldn't speak to her kid! / A four-year-old fucking kid.

ALEX. Stop swearing! For God's sake, Liam, can't you see, everyone's *here*.

BEA *is standing in the corner of the room. Stranded-looking. Adrift.*

BEA. What's happening? What's happened?

KATE. It's okay, we can sort this out. Nothing is / un-sort-out-able.

BEA. I have no idea what's happening.

ALEX (*to* KATE). Is she okay?

KATE. Okay. Let's. Come and sit down, Bea.

BEA. Help me, oh God, what am I doing?

ALEX. Has she taken something?

KATE. Dewi, get a glass of water. Dewi's getting you a glass of water, Bea, come on, sit down.

BEA (*rising panic*). I don't want to sit down. I don't want to come on. Where am I? Where am I?

KATE. At our house. Bea.

ALEX. At Kate's house. With all of us.

BEA (*voice rising*). I don't mean that! Where *am* I? Where have I gone? Oh please God, someone!

KATE. You're here. You're safe. / With us.

BEA (*voice rising*). No! Not that! I'm not with you. I'm on my own. You're all grabbing at me all the time, sniffing around, telling me what I should be doing. Telling me what to *feel*! I don't feel any of that stuff! I can't do it.

ALEX. Do what? / You don't have to do anything.

BEA. Why isn't anyone listening to me?

KATE. We are listening to you. You're panicking, you're disorientated, you're thousands of miles away from, you're separated from your children, it's not natural, / of course you're upset.

BEA. I don't *feel* any of those things!

KATE. Of course you *feel* them. You're suffering because you're *repressing* your feelings, you're in denial. Of course you *feel* them!

BEA. I can't feel anything! I can't do it! I'm shit at it! I'm mean and resentful and bitter and spiteful, I am totally *separate*. I'm broken off, I'm one person and they're three people. I mess everything up. Simon's so good at it all. All the over and over again of it, he knows what to do. We talk about

nothing, I'm just killing time until the children are asleep.
Oh please God, fall asleep! Stay asleep!

Alex, *you know*. You used to say, when the boys were little,
you were just constantly desperate for them to go to sleep
and leave you alone.

ALEX. Not leave me alone –

BEA. Yes you did, you used to say that! You used to say you
had never been so bored in your life, how *awful* it was –

ALEX. Not *awful*. God, it's fucking hard, let's not pretend, but
there's all the good stuff as well. / All the happy. Listen, Bea.

BEA. What good stuff? You said you feared for their safety
sometimes. / Why isn't anyone listening to me?

ALEX. No I didn't! / It gets easier.

BEA. You did! You got so frustrated with Benji that time in the
holiday cottage, you pushed him through that glass door.

ALEX. That was a complete accident! / Oh my God, Bea!

KATE. Listen, you don't have to be a perfect mother. Okay?
I'm not. Alex isn't. Okay? No one is. There's no point in.
You just have to be good *enough*. A good *enough* mother.

BEA. Bollocks.

ALEX. Sorry, everyone, can I just say. Bea, I love you and
everything and I know you are having a really difficult time
and everything but –

BEA. You don't take your child to a good enough doctor, do
you? Oh yes, you can operate on my child, you're good
enough. Oh yes, I'm looking for a good *enough* childminder,
you'll do. You're not great but you're good *enough*. Here's a
good *enough* school, in you go.

ALEX. For fuck's sake. That glass-door thing was a complete
and total –

BEA. Why would anyone aspire to being a good *enough*
mother? –

KATE. Of course I'm not saying *aspire* to be that, / do your
best, of course.

BEA. The world is full of the carnage left behind by substandard mothers.

KATE. Oh fucking fine then! Just walk away!

ALEX. That door, okay, had been open *all* day, okay.

BEA. Simon's brilliant at it. He's the best. I want the best for Kalan and Jay. Why should their childhood be full of me?

KATE. Because that's life. That's what it is. We muddle through. It's all part of a bigger picture. You get a bit wrong, then you get a bit right. Perfection's not a model for anything useful. That's how our children learn, through our failings, they learn to manage, they learn to live realistically in the world. They learn to cope with disappointment and damage.

BEA. That's just waffle to make you feel better for being shit. Why should they? Why should they live with my disappointment and damage? My resentment of them? My wishing that I was somewhere else entirely.

KATE. What do you want me to say? Fair enough, you might as well leave them to it. It sounds a bit shit, it's probably not your cup of tea, move on, best thing. It's not a *job*! You can't give it a go and decide you don't like it. There's a whole load of people's lives! All tangled up with yours!

BEA. I know! I have to get out!

ALEX. Sorry, can I just clarify what happened in Kent, please. Since my son is actually here.

BEA. Come on, Alex, just be honest. You lost your temper, you lashed out, you pushed him into the glass door, / I'm not saying you *meant* to hurt him –

ALEX. I thought I was pushing him out into the garden! Down a tiny, minute little step! I didn't know someone had closed the door, that door had been open the *whole* holiday, I didn't. For fuck's sake, Bea! Do not take me down with you.

DEWI. Leave it.

ALEX. She's making out I'm some kind of / violent maniac! I definitely thought the door was open.

DEWI. Don't rise to it, we were there, remember.

ALEX. Vinnie wasn't.

VINNIE. It's alright, darlin', don't stress.

ALEX. She's making it look. It didn't shatter, there was a crack
but it didn't smash. Did it, Kate?

KATE. No, it didn't.

ALEX. I felt *terrible* about it.

DEWI. We know you did, it's okay.

ALEX. Vinnie doesn't.

VINNIE. It's cool. I know you didn't mean to push a small
child through a plate-glass door.

ALEX. Thank you, Vinnie. Thank you.

Silence.

BEA. Why won't any of you trust me to do the best / thing for
my children?

KATE (*calm*). Because it's not the best thing for them. Your
argument is totally ludicrous. We all think you are making a
grotesque and devastating error of monumental proportions.
How can you think that *not* having a mother is preferable to
having a mother that gets it a bit wrong sometimes. A mother
that struggles, and makes mistakes, sure, who doesn't? But a
mother who loves her children and is interested in them and
has nothing but good intentions, and optimism and hope for
them, supporting them in everything they do, what child
would choose to live without that?

Pause.

BEA. What about a mother who doesn't feel all those things?

Pause.

KATE. What do you mean?

BEA. What about a mother who has waited and waited for those
feelings to come, but they never have. She just struggles and
makes mistakes. Full stop. No interest. No hope. No love.
What about the children of that mother?

Pause.

KATE. Are you saying that's the case for Kalan and Jay?

BEA *says nothing*.

Are you saying you have no feelings of love for Kalan and Jay?

Silence.

VINNIE. You alright, Liam?

LIAM. Yeah.

VINNIE. Good man. (*Pause*.) Do you want a cheese toastie, Liam? I'm going to make a cheese toastie if you're interested.

LIAM. Yeah, alright.

VINNIE. Nice one. Come on then.

VINNIE *goes into the kitchen. After a moment*. LIAM *follows him*.

Silence.

KATE. Bea?

Pause.

DEWI. Okay. This is what we're going to do. Kate. Take Liam's bedding up to Bea's room. Bea, you can sleep in here. If you want to call home, in private. Without an audience. You can do that –

BEA. I don't want to.

DEWI. And if you don't. That's fine too. It's entirely up to you. Bring the duvet down from Bea's bed, Kate. The sofa's comfortable, you'll be fine here. Alex, go to bed. Liam's fine.

KATE *starts to gather up the bedding from the sofa*.

Okay. All good.

ALEX. Let me do that. Don't you do that, Kate. I'll sort Liam out, go back to bed.

KATE. It's fine. I'll just swap this over and then I'll go to bed.

ALEX. Stop it. I can sort my own son's bed out.

DEWI *exits*.

KATE. Okay. Well. Goodnight then.

ALEX. Yeah. Night.

KATE. Goodnight, Bea.

BEA. Goodnight.

ALEX. Goodnight, Bea.

BEA. Goodnight.

ALEX *kisses* BEA *and exits*.

KATE. I'll bring the duvet down from your bed, Bea, and then I'll leave you to it.

BEA. Okay.

KATE. We'll talk in the morning. When you've had a proper rest.

BEA. Okay.

KATE. Right then.

KATE *exits*.

BEA *sits*.

BEA *is on her own*.

Blackout.

Scene Seven

DEWI *and* KATE*'s bedroom.*

Early morning. DEWI *and* KATE *in bed.*

They talk in hushed tones.

KATE. There's a crack in the ground we're all standing on, everything's tipping in.

DEWI. We have to hold on.

KATE. I always thought we were strong.

DEWI. We are.

KATE. It's all so fragile.

DEWI. We're strong.

KATE. What's going to happen to us, Dewi? What's going to happen to Iris?

DEWI. We're going to stick together. We're going to work through it. Nothing bad is going to happen. Nothing bad is going to happen to Iris.

Pause.

KATE. I know you've been in contact with the band.

DEWI. I know you know.

KATE. I know you met up when you were in Cardiff.

DEWI. I know.

KATE. Did you go to Paul's house?

DEWI. No, we met in a restaurant.

KATE. Which one?

DEWI. Sadlers.

KATE. Where's that?

DEWI. Behind Pizza Express.

KATE. Why didn't you go to Pizza Express?

DEWI. Because Paul wanted to meet in Sadlers.

KATE. How do you know I know?

DEWI. Because I know you. (*Pause*.) I'm sorry I didn't tell you.

KATE. It's okay. (*Pause*.) Were you going to tell me?

DEWI. Probably. I don't know.

KATE. Were you frightened of how I'd react?

DEWI. You're so suspicious.

KATE. I'm not suspicious.

DEWI. Jealous.

KATE. Well, are you surprised?

DEWI. You're jealous of everyone though. You're jealous of people that follow me on Twitter.

KATE. They make me feel anxious.

DEWI. It's a madness.

KATE. I know. It's a control issue.

DEWI. Yes. It is.

Pause.

KATE. Dewi.

DEWI. What?

KATE. I am so sorry for stopping you from having a relationship with Sue's baby. I am truly sorry. It was wrong.

DEWI. *What?*

KATE. I was terrified. It's my only defence. It was a terrible thing I did and last night. With Liam. I saw it.

DEWI *cries*.

Whatever you want to do. I'll support you. If you want to send money. Or meet her. Whatever you think is right.

DEWI. I don't know what's right. It's so late. It's too late.

KATE. It's not too late. It's not. Dewi, please. It's not too late to make it right. I'll support you.

DEWI. She'll hate me. She'll never forgive me. It's better to stay away.

KATE. No it's not. She will forgive you. Why don't you think about it? Think of what's best for you and her. I support you. Me and Iris support you. I should never have let you turn your back, it's my fault, I was terrified of her. Just the fact of her. You having a life away from me. I couldn't get past it. Well, I just want you to know that I'm past it now. I forgive you.

Pause.

DEWI. How do we do this?

KATE. We're strong.

DEWI. Are we?

KATE. Yes.

DEWI. Are we strong enough?

KATE. Yes.

DEWI. Such a mess.

Silence.

KATE. It's all held together with these invisible, unspoken, undefinable, conditions. But they're our conditions. We can change them whenever we like.

Silence.

DEWI. Do you think you can still be happy with me, Kate?

KATE. Yes.

DEWI. Are you?

KATE. Yes.

DEWI. And when you look into the future, do you see us?

KATE. Yes, You, me, and Iris. (*Pause.*) And whatever else is happening. (*Pause.*) Shall I tell you when I was happiest?

DEWI. When?

KATE. When we lived in Locke Street and I had that week off work because the office was flooded.

DEWI. You were happiest before we had Iris?

KATE. Listen. We had just started IVF and I felt so positive, so sure it was going to work, so full of hope and clarity about the future. So relieved that we were setting out on a journey together. And you were in your painting trousers –

DEWI. What was I painting?

KATE. Nothing, you were mending the back door because it had swollen in the rain, and you were mending it and I was drinking decaffeinated tea in preparation for being pregnant (I didn't know it would take eight years, ha ha, such ignorant bliss) and I felt properly, deeply, consciously happy.

DEWI. You felt the happiest you have ever felt drinking decaffeinated tea while I mended a door?

KATE. Yes.

DEWI. Bloody hell. (*Pause.*) We've been to Bali! We saw that solar eclipse!

KATE. I know.

DEWI. Bloody hell.

KATE. I know.

There is a knock on their door.

Hello?

ALEX *enters in running gear with two cups of tea.*

ALEX (*whispering*). Hello. I've brought you tea in bed.

KATE. Oh, how lovely! What a treat! Dewi! Can you believe it?

DEWI. Is it decaffeinated?

ALEX. Sorry, have I walked straight into something? Shall I go again?

KATE. No. No, it's fine, come in.

Oh my God, have you been jogging?

ALEX. No, I was going to but I got distracted by two things. Bea's gone.

KATE. What?

ALEX. Yes, she left about fifteen minutes ago, a taxi came and she got in it. I saw through the window. There's no note or anything. I texted her but she hasn't texted me back.

KATE. Oh shit.

ALEX. I know. Without saying goodbye.

KATE. Oh no.

ALEX. I know.

KATE. Shit. (*Pause*.) What was the second thing?

ALEX. Liam suddenly announced he's got a music exam. He needs to be at his teacher's house, with his oboe, for eight. So I'm going to have to drive him there now on three hours' sleep.

KATE. You're not going to get there for eight.

ALEX. I know. The exam's not till nine thirty but he has a practice class, I don't bloody know, he'll just have to be late. *C'est la vie*. Can you believe that baby is still sleeping? Through all of this?

KATE. She sleeps through anything. Seven till seven.

ALEX. She's a miracle child.

KATE. Gina Ford. She goes out like a light.

ALEX. You are so fucking lucky, do not ever underestimate how fucking lucky you are. *None* of mine, not one of them, *ever* went out like a fucking light. Like a furious wild animal that I was trying to wrestle to the ground and shoot with a tranquilliser gun more like. (*Pause*.) I am so sorry about Liam.

KATE. It's fine.

ALEX. Sorry, Dewi.

DEWI. Stop saying sorry.

ALEX. It's okay for the others. At least they've got someone else, sort of, every other weekend. But for Liam, y'know, it's just him and me.

DEWI. He's a great kid.

KATE. They're all great kids. We are so lucky. Do you ever think, look at all these people we've created? And Nat's two. Imagine if we lined them all up in a long line –

ALEX. And shot them!

KATE. No! Alex!

ALEX. Sorry! I just pictured this firing squad and all our poor children!

KATE. Spoiling it.

ALEX. Sorry!

KATE. And just looked at them. Lined them up in height order.

ALEX. Aaaah. Little Iris propped up at the end.

KATE. And just took a moment to look at them. We just need to keep Kalan and Jaybird in the line with everyone else. (*Jumps up.*) Oh my God!

ALEX. What?

KATE. Hang on.

KATE *exits.*

DEWI. Have you listened to any news?

ALEX. No, what's happening?

DEWI. Unbelievable damage. High streets full of smashed-up shops. Burnt-out buildings. It raged all night.

ALEX. Vinnie said they're calling the army in.

DEWI. The police were outnumbered.

ALEX. Can you believe Lewisham Council sent me that text?

DEWI. Major clean-up operation today.

ALEX. Have you got any ibuprofen?

DEWI. Kitchen drawer. Or if not, under the sink in the blue loo.

ALEX. Pounding head.

DEWI. So much anger, simmering away so close to the surface. It's like it's seized its moment to bubble up and burst out.

ALEX. It's frightening.

DEWI. And liberating.

ALEX. Frightening and liberating. That could be the name of your next album.

KATE *enters with a piece of paper.*

KATE. Dewi, did you print out two copies of the flight details?

DEWI. Yeah.

KATE. You printed two copies yeah?

DEWI. Yeah, I did what you said.

ALEX. Has she taken one?

KATE. I think so yes. If Dewi printed out two copies, she's taken one.

DEWI. I did.

KATE. Well, she's definitely taken one then.

ALEX. That's good isn't it.

KATE. That's really good, yes.

ALEX. Well done, Kate.

KATE. Well, let's see. Fingers crossed. I'm going to call Nat.

DEWI. It's ten to seven.

KATE. Oh yes.

ALEX. That's a positive sign, though, isn't it. That she's taken one.

KATE. Yes. It's a positive sign. Do you think, Dewi?

DEWI. Yes.

KATE. Liam's waiting in the car, by the way.

ALEX. Oh! Is he? Okay, better make a move.

    ALEX *stands*.

KATE. He's studying the A to Z. He said you have no sense of direction.

ALEX. I don't!

KATE. I know!

ALEX. Spend half my life driving around lost.

KATE. Well, Liam's in charge of the map.

ALEX. Thank God, at least one of us knows where we're going.

    ALEX *and* KATE *leave the room*.

    DEWI *sits in bed drinking his tea*.

    (*Offstage*.) I have absolutely no idea where I put my phone.

KATE (*offstage*). It's in the kitchen.

ALEX (*offstage*). Oh yes.

    KATE *re-enters*.

KATE. Are you okay?

DEWI. Yes.

KATE. I can hear Iris is awake.

DEWI. Okay. Shall I do nappy and you do porridge?

KATE. I'll do nappy. Shall I bring her in and come back to bed for a bit before porridge?

DEWI. Okay.

    KATE *exits*.

    DEWI *gets up*.

    DEWI *goes into the ensuite bathroom*.

    ALEX *enters*.

ALEX. Oh! He's disappeared!

> ALEX *exits*.

> (*Offstage*.) Where's Dewi?

KATE (*offstage*). In bed.

ALEX (*offstage*). No he's not.

> (*To a baby*.) Oh look! Hello, darling! Hello, beautiful! Oh, Kate, she's so gorgeous. You are so lucky to have a girl one. I got three horrible boys, didn't I? Yes I did! Not lovely and sweet like you, are they? Look at her hair! Oh, I don't want to go now!

KATE (*offstage*). Liam's got an exam.

ALEX (*offstage*). I know.

> *The voices move out of our earshot. The bedroom is empty.*

> *The sound of the toilet flushing.*

> *Lighting change.*

> *Bathroom door opens.* BEA *enters in a T-shirt holding a see-through plastic bag with toiletries in it.*

> BEA *starts to put on clothes thrown over the back of a chair.*

> SIMON *enters the room.*

SIMON. I didn't one hundred per cent understand what she said but I think there's a ninety-minute delay. The Korean guy with the shoes was at reception and he said he's going back to departures now, so I think we should just go.

BEA. Did you want to use my toothpaste?

SIMON. Oh yeah.

BEA. It's on the sink.

SIMON. Okay, thanks.

> *Pause.*

> SIMON *comes into the room and closes the door.*

> Are you okay?

BEA. Yes. Are you?

SIMON. Yes. I'm really okay. I feel really good actually.

BEA. Oh. Good.

SIMON. Do you, I don't want to be pushy, I don't want to scare
you off. Fuck it, listen, you are one of the nicest strangers
I've ever had the good fortune to spend the night with. Do
you want to, you know, hook up, when we get to Melbourne,
for a meal or a… You know, when you're settled in, when
you know what you're doing and stuff. Maybe.

BEA. Yeah. Okay. Definitely.

SIMON. I don't know, it just feels good. Doesn't it? Do you
feel okay about this?

BEA. Yeah, It feels good.

SIMON. I don't know, I've been in enough situations to know
what feels, not necessarily situations like this, I don't want
you to think I'm forever staying in hotels with women I meet
on planes –

BEA. I believe you.

SIMON. This just feels right.

BEA. Okay.

SIMON. And I could show you round Melbourne, I'd love to, I
don't know, be your guide.

BEA. Okay.

SIMON. Yeah?

BEA. Yeah. I'd like that. I'd like you to be my guide.

SIMON. Okay, that's great.

BEA. I'd like that.

SIMON. I'd like that too. Cos, you know, you live in a city, all
your life, and you go to work and come home, and you stop
seeing it somehow. And I'm an architect! I spend all day
thinking about buildings. But when you introduce someone
else to the place you live you see stuff again. I'd love to
share that experience with you, if you're okay with that.

BEA. That sounds perfect. Because, I'm a long way from home.

SIMON *moves towards* BEA *and holds out his hand to her. She takes it.*

SIMON. I'd love to walk with you and see where it takes us.

BEA. Okay. I'd be up for that.

I'll embark on an adventure with you.

Blackout.

The End.

www.nickhernbooks.co.uk

facebook.com/nickhernbooks

twitter.com/nickhernbooks